CENOTE SALLY'S

EASY, BREEZY TROPICAL LIVING

HUNDREDS OF TIPS THAT WILL SAVE YOU THOUSANDS OF DOLLARS

EUNICE "CENOTE SALLY" WENTWORTH

Copyright © 2013 by Hispanic Economics, Inc.

Manufactured in the United States of America. All rights reserved. No part of this book may be reproduced in any form or by any means, electronic or mechanical, including photocopying, recording, or by information storage, and retrieval systems—except by a reviewer who may quote brief passages in a review to be printed in a magazine, newspaper or on the Internet—without permission in writing from the publisher.

Although the author and publisher have made every good faith effort to ensure the accuracy and completeness of information contained in this book, we assume no responsibility for errors, inaccuracies, omissions or inconsistencies herein. This book is presented solely for educational and entertainment purposes. The advice offered is provided for educational purposes and it is not offered as professional services advice. The opinions expressed are solely those of the author and do not necessarily reflect the opinions of the publisher, its employees or affiliates.

This book is published by Hispanic Economics, Inc. It expresses solely the personal opinions, conclusions, and recommendations of the author. No liability is assumed for damages resulting from the use of information contained herein.

First printing 2013
Publication date: December 2013.

ATTENTION CORPORATIONS, UNIVERSITIES, COLLEGES, and PROFESSIONAL AND CHARITABLE ORGANIZATIONS: Quantity discounts are available on bulk purchases of this book for educational and gift purposes, or as premiums in fundraising efforts. Inquiries should be sent to info@hispaniceconomics.com.
Hispanic Economics, Inc.
P.O. Box 140681
Coral Gables, FL 33114-0681

info@hispaniceconomics.com
HispanicEconomics.com

ISBN 978-1-939879-07-3

Cover and Interior Design by John Clifton
john@johnclifton.net

CONTENTS

Introduction 1

Wonderful Uses for Vinegar! 4

Vermouth Panaché 9

Wonderful Uses for Baking Soda! 10

Gin & Tonic 15

Wonderful Uses for Lemons! 16

White Lady 22

Wonderful Laundry Tips! 23

Gimlet 31

Wonderful Tips for your Terrace and Garden! 32

Classic Daiquiri 44

Wonderful Tips for Removing Stains! 45

Campari & Gin 52

Wonderful Tips for Entertaining! 53

Martini 64

Wonderful Beauty Tips! 65

Sangria 77

Wonderful Pet Care Tips! 78

Negroni 86

Wonderful Everyday Household & Car Tips! 87

Pernod Cocktail 100

Wonderful Tips for a Good Night's Sleep! 101

Tea 103

Epilogue 104

Adios, Mi Vida 105

About the Author 106

INDEX 108

INTRODUCTION

It all began when we set sail from what today is known as Marina Hemingway, east of Havana, Cuba, for points unknown. It was February 1960, just a year after the *Revolución*. There were misgivings in the air. My dear husband, who loathed Fulgencio Batista, had initially welcomed what promised to be a democratic change for that beautiful island nation.

One day, however, he came home, visibly upset, and said, "We have to leave this place. Nothing here will turn out well."

The only times he was ever upset was when he went out for drinks with friends who were surreptitious spies for the Central Intelligence Agency, or the CIA, of which Latin America has always been awash. He didn't say much more and I never inquired, respecting his judgment.

We quietly settled our affairs with friends and colleagues. All was concluded a few short weeks after his initial announcement. After a farewell dinner at the Hotel Nacional we made our way back to our sailboat. We set sail for Progreso, Yucatán. It was a magnificent tropical night. We never looked back.

It was our intention to sail to Campeche, then Veracruz, and finally to New Orleans. But, arriving in Yucatán, we were enchanted by this beautiful land.

This is how we rediscovered the gorgeous city of Mérida. After months of renting a gracious home in Mérida proper, we settled on purchasing an abandoned hacienda—shambles it was! But we were up for the adventure of rebuilding it, room by room, section by section. It was a difficult undertaking. There were no Home Depot or Boxito stores around the corner. We had to find our own architects, masons, carpenters, electricians, and plumbers.

As much a labor of love as it was an act of determination, from the ruins, we build a gracious home. In the process I learned to fend for myself and find solutions to everyday problems. How do you keep insects out of your terrace? What's the best way of removing stains from linens? How can books be kept safe from mildew? Is there an easy remedy to keep ants out of the kitchen? What can one do about wasp nests? Mosquitoes? Scorpions?

In small, lined spiral notebooks I compiled one solution and remedy at a time. And these spiral notebooks are the source for the hundreds of tips that will save you thousands of dollars as you enjoy an Easy, Breezy life in whichever warm, tropical environment you have chosen for yourself!

I will also provide the answer to the most often-asked question. Yes, in due course I will divulge how I came to be called "Cenote Sally"!

It's all here, gentle reader, in due course!

Eunice "Cenote Sally" Wentworth
Hacienda Escondido
Off the Hunucmá-Sisal Road
Yucatán State, Mexico

This book is for Concepción Caamal, who has taken care of us faithfully and whom we have endeavored to take care of as well. With all my yaaj. . . amor . . . love!

WONDERFUL USES FOR VINEGAR!

Did I tell you?

When we first moved to Yucatán—decades before NAFTA—there was no hope of finding a Sam's Club or Costco anywhere. Getting imported goods was a hit-or-miss adventure!

My goodness! It involved almost . . . smuggling . . . and indeed, it *was* smuggling!

We had to trek downtown to the vast market near the Museum of the City. Back then that building really was the Main Post Office and the Telegram Office. Yes, we did send telegrams—and receive telegrams. They were messages like: "Arriving Tuesday, the 17th. STOP. Pan Am flight from Miami. STOP. Nancy & Kenneth. STOP."

Nancy, of course, was Nancy Keith, who once was married to the director Howard Hawks. When she visited us in Yucatán she was married to Kenneth Keith and was well on her way to becoming Lady Keith! No one ever called her Nancy, however. It was always Slim.

Slim, of course, thought Yucatán was a land of staggering beauty. So did Kenneth. Obviously, both had discerning eyes.

As I said, we had to journey to the *mercado* across the street from the present-day Museum of the City for . . . *goods from other countries*. The area of the market with the contraband merchandise was called "El Chetumalito," since these goods were smuggled from Belize. Belize was British Honduras back then. From British Honduras truckloads made their way into Chetumal, Mexico and then overland to Mérida.

British Honduras was a more integrated member of the Commonwealth nations. Goods from all the former British colonies and the United Kingdom flowed freely. Maple syrup from Canada, wines from South Africa, bolts of fabulous cloths from London! And wonderful cheeses—Dutch Gouda and English Stilton! It was a plethora of exquisite merchandise. And it was certainly an expedition to explore *El Chetumalito*.

Darling, what a treat it was to get my hands on Wood Dunn Dairy Maid butter from New Zealand!

And, of course, there were always the clandestine deliveries from friends who sailed to Yucatán from Key Largo or Key West . . . memories!

But enough about me and my nostalgia for outlaw days, let's move on to the matter at hand!

White Vinegar to the Rescue!

Welcome Home!

If you're a snowbird who has just returned to the tropics, pour a little bit of vinegar in a cup and place in front of your air conditioner. As the vinegar evaporates and circulates throughout the room it will act as a natural air freshener!

New Jeans

When you unpack, if you bought yourself new jeans, here's an old trick. Wash them in the rinse cycle—but add one cup of vinegar instead of fabric softener. This will soften the jeans—and make them colorfast, so you won't have a concern going forward.

Kitchen Knives

Knives will cut better if you soak them in vinegar, one cup vinegar to one cup warm water, for about half an hour. Then simply rinse and the knives will be sharper than ever before.

Kitchen Sponges

Done with the knives? Don't throw that solution away—at least not before you soak your kitchen sponges first! After 15 minutes, rinse the vinegar out. The sponges will be much cleaner.

Jewelry Cleaner

A simple way to rid jewelry of sunscreen or other lotions applied to your skin is simple: soak them for a few minutes in a solution of warm water and white vinegar: 1/5 cup vinegar and ½ cup warm water should do it. Then rinse your jewelry thoroughly.

Easy Shower Cleaning

Combine one part white vinegar and eight parts tap water. Pour into a spray bottle. That's all you need to have a handy solution to fight hard water buildup in your shower. Just keep the spray bottle handy and spray after you shower. Do this and you will keep your shower so much cleaner!

Clean Your Hair

As long as you're in the shower, the best way of degreasing your hair is with vinegar. Shampoo as normal. Then pour 1/5 cup vinegar over your hair and rinse once more.

Extend the Life of your Propane Lantern

If you soak the wick the day before you use your propane lantern you will extend the life of your wick twice as long. That was easy!

Eliminate Kitchen Smells

Is the smell of garlic—or worse yet, something burnt—stinking up your kitchen? The solution is simple: one cup vinegar and two cups water. Boil. After ten minutes of boiling the vinegar will absorb the unwelcome smell.

Now for Dishwasher Smells

In the tropics, all kinds of things grow inside the dishwasher. This is why it's important to run your dishwasher on the RINSE cycle once a week. Be sure to pour vinegar where the detergent goes and you will not only clean properly your dishwasher, but your glassware will come out even cleaner than before.

And your Washing Machine . . .

Will wash better if you pour in a cup of vinegar and run on the rinse cycle. The vinegar will remove the alkaline residue that builds up over time, especially in climates with hard water!

Cleaning Ceiling Fans

Cleaning ceiling fans is simple enough: one cup vinegar and one cup water makes a great solution. But here's a trick: polish with a fabric softener. That will reduce the amount of dust that accumulates!

Clean Those T-Shirts!

Let's face it: deodorants and perspiration tend to yellow your T-shirt underarms—and that's unsightly! One solution is to soak the underarm areas in vinegar for about 15 minutes. Then throw in the washing machine as usual. Do this habitually and you will keep your T-shirts from getting yellow underarms stains.

Coffee and Grass Stains

After a glorious breakfast on the terrace . . . what's that? You ended up with coffee or grass stains on yourself? Try soaking gently the stained area with vinegar and that coffee or grass stain should rinse away without a problem!

Gum Stuck on Fabric?

Warm half a cup of vinegar and, using a toothbrush, saturate the gum. Then slowly brush it out. It should work on most fabrics.

Suede Stains

Stains can be removed—especially if you catch them when they first occur—with a combination of vinegar and patience. Dip a toothbrush in vinegar and most grease stains can then be removed from suede. Really!

Ease Wasp Stings

Surprised by news of guests arriving from New England? Nothing I can do about that, but on the other hand, if you were stung by a wasp—of the insect variety, here's a solution. Use a cotton ball to dab the area with cider vinegar and you will find relief.

Label Remover

If you saturate a price label with white vinegar, you will then be able to peel it off without leaving any sticky residue!

Spiffy Flower Pots

Those plastic flower pots will look like new if you soak them in your kitchen sink using this ratio: one cup vinegar to two cups water. Make sure the water is warm!

Speaking of Potted Plants?

Were we? When you are reusing those pots, if you add one cup vinegar to one gallon water, you can use this solution to increase the acidity in the soil—and plants love that. Rinse those pots in this solution! Why? Vinegar allows the natural iron in the soil to be released, which plants need to flourish!

Tar Removal

In the tropics, tar often warms up and it winds up on your sandals, sneakers and even the bottom of your pants, jeans, and trousers. A solution is at hand! A few drops of vinegar is all you need to remove these tar stains!

End Fruit Fly Infestation

Fruit flies can be a nuisance. Here's a solution: pour cider vinegar in a small bowl—and add a couple of drops of dishwashing detergent. The vinegar attracts the flies. The detergent breaks the surface tension, so the flies drown.

Princess is Parched!

And I am confident you could use a potent potable just about right now. I think I'll have a . . .

VERMOUTH PANACHÉ

2 ounces French (dry) vermouth
1 ounce Italian (sweet) vermouth
1 dash Angostura bitters

Fill a tall glass with ice, add ingredients. Wait a moment, stir, and garnish with a lemon peel.

Read "A Farewell to Arms," the novel by Ernest Hemingway. In Chapter 35 the Vermouth Panaché is referenced when Henry and Emilio, after a failed fishing trip, share a vermouth drink. But of course you knew that, didn't you?

Drink and read . . . responsibly!

WONDERFUL USES FOR BAKING SODA!

Did I tell you?

The other day I glanced at the mirror's reflection and I saw myself in the harsh morning light of summer in Yucatán. It is an unforgiving light. I looked like Gloria Stuart, as Gloria Stuart looked playing the whacked out old lady in *Titanic*.

Why do I say she was whacked out?

Darling, only someone who is not playing with a full set is demented enough, at the end of the film, to toss a set of priceless jewels into the frigid waters of the North Atlantic!

If that nut job had to toss them anywhere, why couldn't she toss them in my swimming pool?

One look in the mirror, however, and I did in fact realize that I have grown old.

My good friend, who asked to remain anonymous since she disagrees with my confessional approach to divulging my Easy, Breezy tips, has encouraged me to seek out male companionship. But when one is as old as I am, what can one do?

Besides, the hottest man in town is taken! Yes, you know who I mean: Carol Kolozs of Rosas & Xocolatl, who else?

Doesn't he always have some gorgeous Mexican beauty by his side? Some divine creature that looks like the stunning Mexican actress Ana de la Reguera? (If you don't know who she is, look her up on YouTube in that amusing commercial for Kahlúa.) That's who his gorgeous girlfriends always look like. How can anyone ever hope to compete?

Despite my protests, however, my friend insists that "online dating" might be the way to go. Really? Match.com? eHarmony.com?

I doubt it.

And unless there is something more age-appropriate for me . . . an old dinosaur . . . Is there? Is there a dating site for old relics like me? A living fossil? If there is, it must have a stupid name . . . like . . . *Carbon Dating Online*!

But enough about me and my silly concerns, let's move on to the matter at hand!

Baking Soda to the Rescue

Jewelry Cleaner

Gold and silver jewelry can be cleaned using a paste of baking soda and hydrogen peroxide. It's true! To a quarter cup hydrogen peroxide add baking soda until you achieve a pasty, watery consistency that you can use to clean your jewelry. Good-bye Tarn-X or other harsh (and expensive) cleaners!

Clean Breath

One cup water, ½ teaspoon salt and ½ teaspoon baking soda is all you need to make a mouth wash. Gargle, rinse, and you won't need Scope or Listerine.

Clean Hair

If you add ¼ teaspoon baking soda to the normal amount of shampoo you use and shampoo as normal, filmy residue in your hair will rinse away!

Cooking Beans?

If you simply add a sprinkle of baking soda to beans as they are cooking you will reduce the gases produced in your body afterwards! Good riddance to flatulence!

Freshen up Area Rugs and Carpets

Equal parts baking soda and corn starch, when sprinkled on area rugs and carpets, will freshen them. Simply sprinkle and leave overnight. Vacuum the next morning!

Germ-Free Combs and Brushes

With a quart hot water and two tablespoons baking soda, you have a great tonic to clean combs and brushes.

Cleaning Stainless Steel

Make a paste of baking soda and vinegar. You now have a perfect cleaner for stainless steel faucets, appliance, counters, and sinks!

Clean with Coffee Grinds and Baking Soda

Here's a trick: used coffee grinds can be poured down the drain—along with a little baking soda—and then let the hot water run. That combination will break down the grease that accumulates in the pipes avoiding trouble down the road.

Hard Water Stains on Dishes

Is hard water causing your dishes to come out with stains? A tablespoon baking soda added during the rinse cycle will solve that problem next time you use your dishwasher.

Cleaning Grout

Three parts baking soda to one part water makes a splendid paste to clean grout between tiles. An old toothbrush is the other thing you need.

Kitchen Counter

Rather than using Comet or some other abrasive, use baking soda with warm water and a sponge as a scouring powder for kitchen counters.

Unclog that Drain!

A simple solution for unclogging drains is to pour one cup baking soda, one cup salt, and ½ cup white vinegar. Simple chemistry will do a fine job of breaking down grease and organic material. Then flush with hot water! Who needs Drano?

Baking Soda . . . and Fresher Vegetables

Of course you know that a box of baking soda in the refrigerator absorbs odors, but did you know that if you soak a brand new sponge in a solution of warm water and baking soda and place it where cheeses and cold cuts are kept, these will keep fresher longer? Now you do!

Meat Tenderizer

Generously sprinkling baking soda on tougher cuts of meat will tenderize them in no time. Simply rinse thoroughly after pounding the meat and season as normal.

Extending the Life of Milk

Add a pinch of baking soda to a carton of milk. It will stay fresher for about a week past its expiration date!

Clean Coffee Makers

If you combine ¼ cup baking soda to one quart water and run through your coffee maker as if you were making coffee—guess what? You'll clean the coffee maker so the next time you do make coffee, it will taste better!

Clean Blenders and Food Processors

One tablespoon baking soda and one cup warm water is all that you need to clean the blades of your blender or food processor. Pour this solution in either a blender or food processor. Run for 15 seconds. Then clean as usual.

Fresher Garbage Cans

Generously sprinkling baking soda at the bottom of a garbage can will greatly reduce odors!

A Remedy for Mildewed Suitcases

Sprinkle baking soda in your mildewed suitcase, shake, and set aside overnight. The next day, vacuum the baking soda!

Painted Surfaces

Pencil and crayon marks on painted surfaces can be easily removed using baking soda and a damp cloth. Rub and then rinse.

Crystal Clear

Baking soda and warm water create a fine solution for cleaning cut crystal with a soft rag. Rinse with water and then, when dry, you can buff with a soft, dry cloth.

No Curdles in Your Milk

A pinch of baking soda added to milk you are about to heat up will prevent it from curdling.

Is there too Much Chlorine in the Pool?

Simple solution: pour in baking soda until the pH balance is restored!

Freshen Vacuum Cleaners

Simply sprinkle baking soda into your vacuum cleaner bag and it will smell fresher!

Cleaning Plastic Containers

By simply rinsing clear plastic storage containers with warm water and 2-3 tablespoons baking soda, they will be fresh as new.

Fresh-Smelling Cars

If your car is equipped with an ashtray, then fill it with baking soda—not ashes! It will keep your car smelling fresh. And the baking soda is easy to vacuum away. Good-bye pine-cone scented air fresheners!

Oil Stains on Driveways

If you have an oil stain on your garage floor or driveway, sprinkle baking soda. Then scrub with a utility brush and hot water. Hose clean!

Freshen Guests Bedroom

Guests arriving and the guest bedroom smells stale? Sprinkle baking soda on the mattress and pillows—and then dress with fresh bedding and pillow cases!

Cleaning Fiberglass

If you have fiberglass furniture for your patio, the question arises: How do you keep it looking new in this tropical climate? Here's an easy solution—but not for the faint of heart! Outdoors, or in a very well ventilated room, mix one cup vinegar, ½ cup baking soda, and ½ cup ammonia to one gallon of water. Using rubber gloves and a sponge designated exclusively for this purpose clean the furniture. Rinse very well. If you spill some on your skin, *immediately* stop what you're doing to rinse. Wash where the ammonia touched your skin in cool running water.

Princess is Parched!

And I am confident you could use a potent potable just about right now. I think I'll have a . . .

GIN & TONIC

2 ounces London dry gin
4 ounces tonic water
2 dashes Angostura bitters

Fill a tall glass with ice, add ingredients. Wait a moment, stir, and garnish with a lime peel.

Read "The Denunciation," a short story by Ernest Hemingway. The gin & tonic is featured prominently in this riveting tale that unfolds at Chicote's bar in Madrid during the Spanish Civil War. But of course you knew that, didn't you?

Drink and read . . . responsibly!

WONDERFUL USES FOR LEMONS!

Did I tell you?

Years back, when we finally had completed our home, and we were in the process of "settling down and settling in" as my husband used to phrase it, we embarked on several adventures.

The one I found most rewarding was trying to "track down" some of the intellectuals in Yucatán. There are quite a number of accomplished intellects in Mérida, mind you. But one of the most endearing, charming, and thoroughly delightful personalities happened to be Miguel Bretos.

Of course, someone of his stature gets "snapped up" just like that, right? In other words, it was easier to track him down at the Smithsonian Institution in Washington, D.C. than it was to find him at his home in town!

Always wearing a lovely bowtie—he is so "Old School" in his charming manners—he reminded us of Irvine R. Levine, our wonderful, splendid, and nerdy friend who was a correspondent for NBC News. If you don't know who he was, Google him!

Darling, I will say Miguel Bretos and Irving R. Levine must have shopped for bowties at the same shops: Brooks Brothers, Paul Stuart or the now-defunct Britches of Georgetowne. I do, however, think that once in a while someone bought them fabulous bowties from Paul Smith or Thomas Pink or Drakes of London!

In any case, of course intellectual giants are always working on some wonderful project or other. I found it a challenge to slug through *Iglesias de Yucatán*, which Miguel Bretos wrote to critical acclaim. The project he was working on recently was a book titled, *Biografía de una Catedral, la gran casa de Dios en medio de Toh*, the history of Mérida's cathedral. It promises to be quite an undertaking.

What initiative on his part, don't you think?

And speaking of my other friend, Irvine R. Levine, here's a tidbit. I'll bet you didn't know he was the first accredited American journalist in the former Soviet Union. Yes, he was. And back then, there were spies everywhere!

He used to tell us that when he was in Moscow, his quarters were bugged by Soviet intelligence. He would entertain American and Latin American guests. Whenever anyone criticized the Soviet system, he was sure to, in a loud voice, stand under the chandelier and pronounce, "As for myself, I think this is a great country and a wonderful system, and this is Irving R. Levine speaking."

Miguel Bretos is the same way, in a manner of speaking, devoting his vast intellectual powers to affirming the good in all of us!

How I love bowties! Say what you will, bowties make wonderful neckwear!

But enough about me and my sartorial recommendations, let's move on to the matter at hand!

Wonderful Tips for Lemons

Scorpions Away!

In tropical climes . . . there are scorpions! One secret I've found that helps is simple: one cup lemon or lime juice and one cup water. Mix in spray bottle. Then spray on your shower floor and terrace areas. Scorpions hate the scent and will not venture forth!

Cleaning Shower Curtains

If you have shower curtains—and there's really no reason you should—one way of preventing mildew from appearing is to soak the curtains in soap and water. Then sponge one cup lime juice and let it dry in the sun. That's the secret to minimizing mildew!

Extend the Life of Shower Curtains

All you have to do is spray your shower curtain with a combination of one cup hydrogen peroxide, ½ cup lemon juice, and water once a week. If you want it to work faster, let the shower curtains dry out in direct sunlight! Works wonders!

Cleaning Copper Cookware

Make a paste with table salt and lime juice. Rub it (with gloves on!) over any copper item in your kitchen. Scrub using a sponge. Rinse and dry.

Clean Coffee Pots, Decanters, and Glass Pitchers

If you use a solution of ¾ cup lime juice and ¼ cup white vinegar, you can make your coffee pot, decanter or glass pitcher sparkle like new!

Freshen Up Wilting Vegetables

If your veggies start to wilt because they've been in the refrigerator too long, here's an Easy, Breezy remedy. Pour ¼ cup lemon or lime juice in a bowl of cool water (a couple of ice cubes helps!). Then soak your carrots, spinach, lettuce, radishes or celery for about 10 or 15 minutes!

Polish Wood Surfaces

For varnished wood surfaces, add three or four drops lime juice to ½ cup warm water. Spray on a damp cloth and wipe furniture. For unvarnished wood surfaces, mix two teaspoons lime juice and two teaspoons olive oil. Using a cotton cloth polish wood, making sure you distribute the solution evenly.

Freshen Garbage Disposal

Cut up a few lemons, grinds and all, and run through the garbage disposal. This will deodorize the disposal, while killing bacteria.

Freshen Rooms

An economical way of freshening any room—especially guests rooms—is using a portable humidifier. Pour ¼ cup lime juice into the water and the scent of mustiness will dissipate in a few hours!

Reduce Dust

A simple way of minimizing dust is easy enough: mix 10 drops lemon or lime juice with a few drops olive oil. Shake vigorously and, using a spray bottle, "dust" surfaces in your kitchen—ceiling fan, top of microwave, refrigerator, or any other surface. The lemon will repel dust particles!

Brighten Kitchen Sinks

Dissolve salt in lime juice and use a damp cloth to wipe down stainless steel and aluminum surfaces. They will shine like new!

Remove Scratches from Wood

A few drops of lime juice and olive oil, using a soft cloth, will do wonders in eliminating light scratches from wood furniture and surfaces.

Keep Painted Surface Insect-Free

For so many years whenever we did patch-up painting, insects would get stuck on the wet paint! Then a Maya friend shared with me her secret: add a few drops of lime juice to the paint, and the bugs will stay away while the paint dries!

Keep Paint Brushes Looking Like New

You can save a small fortune if you bring a cup lemon juice to boil and then dip hardened paintbrushes. Remove from heat and, 15 minutes later, wash the paintbrush in soapy water!

Extend the Life of Guacamole

A few lime drops on guacamole will prevent it from oxidizing—and turning brown!

Keep Apples from Turning Brown

A few drops of lime juice on a cut apple will also prevent oxidation.

Cleaning Brass

Cut a lemon wedge, dip in baking soda, and use this to clean brass. Rub it into the brass surface, let sit for 10 minutes. Rinse and buff dry. Next problem!

Removing Carpet Stains

Baking soda and a few drops of lime juice rubbed into a carpet stain is one solution—provided the carpet is colorfast. If it is, then you can easily remove any organic stain—from wine to fruit juice. Let sit for a few minutes, then wipe with a damp cloth.

Cleaner Glass Windows

A ¼ cup of lemon juice and a sponge is all you need to clean glass. Whether it is a kitchen window, a sliding glass door or the shower glass, it works. Wipe the glass with lemon juice. Then use a soft cloth (or newspaper) to rub dry!

Disinfect Cutting Boards

Bacteria certainly breed! A quick way of disinfecting any cutting board, or other cutting surface, is to pour salt and then use half a lime as a scouring pad. The salt and acidity in the lime will kill off the bacteria.

Cutting Board Stains

Oh, no! Are beet juices staining your cutting board? Quick, reach for a lime. Rub the lime into the stain and let rest for about 15 minutes. Then rinse under cool water!

Fluffier Rice

One tablespoon of lime juice added to water will make rice fluffier—and taste better.

Eliminate Odors

If somehow you spilled an alkaline onto your skin, such as those found in bleaches, then rub lemon. Lemon is acidic and counteracts alkaline! The odor is gone almost instantly. Then wash your hands in cool water.

Clean Ivory

Dissolve enough salt in a ¼ cup lemon juice to make a paste. Gently rub—even piano keys—and then wipe clean with a damp cloth.

Cleaner Toilet

Yes, it's true. Pour a cup of lime juice in your toilet tank, and then flush . . . and this will reduce hard water and clean your toilet from the inside out!

Freshen Microwaves

Too dependent on your microwave? If you are, then you might have odors or stains. A simple solution? Here it is: place a small bowl with tepid water and slices of lemons or limes floating. Microwave for four or five minutes. Remove and then you will be surprised how easily the stains are wiped away with a damp cloth—and your microwave will smell fresh!

Extracting Juice

Speaking of microwaves, did you know that if you place a lime or lemon in the microwave and heat for just 10 or 12 seconds you will then be able to extract that much more juice? Now you do!

Brighten Tennis Shoes

Here's an Easy, Breezy secret: spray lemon juice on your white tennis shoes and leave in the sun. They will whiten—and smell fresh!

Kitchen Counter Cleaned and Bacteria Free

One quarter-cup lemon juice, ¼ cup white vinegar, and ½ cup water is all you need—and a spray bottle. Spray and wipe counters to clean and disinfect surfaces in your kitchen! (Also works great in your bathroom!)

Upset Stomach? No more!

Did you know that if you suck on a lemon you can settle an upset stomach? Now you do!

Natural Insect Repellent!

Before heading out to the terrace or patio for the evening, lightly spray your blouse with a solution of water and lemon juice—the scent of the lemon will keep mosquitoes far away from you!

Princess is Parched!

And I am confident you could use a potent potable just about right now. I think I'll have a . . .

WHITE LADY

1 ½ ounce London dry gin
1 ounce Cointreau
¾ ounce fresh lemon juice

Shake well in a mixing glass with generous amounts of ice. Strain into a chilled cocktail glass.

Read *Islands in the Stream* by Ernest Hemingway. In Chapter 2, Joseph, the houseboy, advises Tom Hudson that the drinks at the house are better than those at Bobby's. "Mr. Bobby was in an evil mood when I went by," Joseph says. "Too many mixed drinks he says. Somebody off a yacht asked him for something called a White Lady." But of course you knew that, didn't you?

Drink and read . . . responsibly!

WONDERFUL LAUNDRY TIPS!

Did I tell you?

There are times when going to Centro is terrifying. Once I was driving in Santiago along Calle 55 when I was stunned to see the apparition of a ghoul. There she was, to my right, meandering along Calle 72!

Emaciated, wearing a Oaxacan embroidered blouse, this ghost, pale and thin, was walking down the street. She was accompanied by her Afghan hound. The creature mouthed the line: "Each and every heart it seems is bounded by a world of dreams."

Her eyes were vacant and her lips were cracked as she mouthed the words. I came to screeching halt and the creature looked straight at me and repeated that phrase several times.

The horror!

There are ghosts in Mérida! I most definitely believe that. I have seen a good number of ghosts. I have heard many stories of friends and visitors who have stumbled upon these creatures.

Darling, I do have to confess that this ghoul scared the shit out of me!

But enough about me and my soiled panties, let's move on to the matter at hand! Laundry!

Save on Detergent

Here's a secret that detergent manufacturers won't tell you: if you half the "recommended" amount of detergent per load, you will still get the same cleaning results. It's true!

Fabric Softeners

In most cases, you can use a fabric softening sheet twice and it is still as potent the second time around!

Easier Washing

Always remove pins or buckles. Zip zippers. But DO NOT button buttons! Doing so can stress the buttonholes. Turn sweaters and T-shirts inside out.

Unfurl socks, unroll cuffs, and empty pockets.

Be Gentle with Delicates

Wash these separately in a mesh bag. Substitute ½ laundry detergent with borax, which has antiseptic, antibacterial, water-softening, and whitening properties.

Let the Sun Whiten Whites!

Hanging whites to dry in the tropical sun will add a brightening boost to your laundry.

Laundering White Napkins

Let these soak overnight in a plastic tub. Pour hot water, a cup each of white vinegar and detergent. Add one medium size lemon, sliced. The next day let the water run until these are thoroughly rinsed. Never wring or squeeze, but place between two white towels and press gently. Let air dry to the point when they are lightly damp. Iron and starch!

When to Hand Wash

Save yourself a small fortune by learning how to hand wash fine washables, including wool, silk, and linen. The technique is to fill a small container with lukewarm water and a mild detergent (shampoo will do!). Immerse delicates and swish for about five minutes. Drain soapy water and rinse until water runs clear. Do not wring. Instead, lay flat on a towel and with another towel press gently. You can also roll to press out excess water. Repeat with another towel and air dry.

Use Dryer Wisely

With so much sunshine in the tropics, why use the dryer for everything? Whites smell and look better when hung to dry in the sun. Pillows and clothes that have been stored away can be "freshened up" by tossing a dryer sheet and running the dryer on AIR FLUFF, which circulates air, but provides no heat. Remove jeans while damp and let them air dry to reduce wrinkles.

Wash Down

Down pillows and other items can be safely washed in the washing machine and then dried in the dryer. Make sure to set the dryer to the tumble-low setting and toss in a couple of tennis balls! This make sure they fluff up as they dry.

Suntan Oil Stain

It happens to everyone, doesn't it? You come back from the beach and you have suntan oil on your swimsuit or other beach garment. The solution? Simple. Soak the article in dishwashing liquid detergent, and let sit for a few hours. Then rinse in cold water.

Gasoline and Petrol Spills

Spilled some gasoline while lighting the night on fire? It's happened to all of us. The solution is simple enough: place the garment in a bucket of cold water, pour in a 12 ounce can of Coke (not Pepsi, not Diet Coke!) and a cup of baking soda. Let it soak overnight. Rinse in cold water in the morning and let air dry. Wash as usual, and the gasoline scent will be long gone.

Protect Fine Linens

How? In the tropics, it's imperative you place a piece of wax paper on top of fine linens. This will protect them from mildew—and fading from strong sunlight.

Whiter than White Towels

How do you keep white towels whiter than white? Launder as usual, but during the rinse cycle add one cup hydrogen peroxide to your washing machine as a substitute for bleach. The result will be whiter than white towels—without damaging the integrity of the fabrics!

Tobacco Smells

Half a cup baking soda added to the wash cycle is a sure way of getting tobacco—cigarettes and cigar—smells out of your laundry.

Salsa Stains

Holy guacamole! That delicious salsa stained your outfit? Quick, run cool water from the back of the fabric. If the fabric is colorfast, use a bleaching agent, such as hydrogen peroxide or white vinegar poured directly on the stain. Then immediately apply a gentle liquid detergent. Launder. If the fabric is not colorfast, after running cool water, launder as instructed on the garment's label.

Syrup Stains

This is one time when you have to resist temptation and rather than running warm water, you must saturate the stain with COLD WATER. Let it sit for five or ten minutes. Then apply a gentle liquid detergent. Then rinse through the back with HOT WATER.

Ketchup

Once again, soak the stained fabric in cold water. Add a gentle liquid dishwashing liquid and softly work into the fabric. If it is colorfast, remove from the water and pour hydrogen peroxide. Let it sit, and rinse. If there is any stain left, add more hydrogen peroxide. If the fabric is NOT colorfast, launder immediately per the garment's instructions.

Saving on Dry Cleaning

To save money—and trips—to the drycleaner, simply hang your blouse, trousers or other item in your bathroom when you are taking a hot shower. The steam should get rid of most wrinkles—and you can always use a steamer (1,200 to 1,500 watts) to steam out the more stubborn wrinkles.

Wine Stains in Laundry

1. After having tested the fabric for colorfastness, try the following remedy.

For white wine, blot as much of the stain as you can. Then pour salt and let it sit overnight. In the morning, the stain should be gone. Launder as usual.

2. After having tested the fabric for colorfastness, try the following remedy. For red wine, blot as much of the stain as you can, mindful not to apply pressure as you work the fabric. Immediately pour hydrogen peroxide. Add a gentle dishwashing liquid. If you have unflavored club soda, pour on the stain. If not, add some more hydrogen peroxide. Immediately launder.

Tea Stains

Guess what? If you spilled tea all over your favorite blouse or shirt . . . the trick is to dab lime juice with a bit of water. Apply to the stain with a cotton squab! Then launder as usual.

Whitening the Whites

As long as you have the lime juice out, add half a cup lime juice to the wash cycle and your whites will be whiter than if you used bleach. That was simple.

Worcestershire Sauce

Blot as much of the stain as you can. Run cold water from the back of the stain. Then pour baking soda on the front of the stain. Let sit for five minutes. Run under cold water again. If the stain is still there, and if the fabric is colorfast, add a few drops of hydrogen peroxide. Then rinse once more. Launder immediately.

Sour Cream Stains

Blot as much of the stain as you can. Run cold water from the back of the stain. Rub a gentle dishwashing liquid detergent and let sit for half an hour. Rinse with cold water. Launder as usual.

Relish Stains

Blot as much of the stain as you can. Run cold water from the back of the stain. Then pour baking soda on the front of the stain. Let sit for five minutes. Run under cold water. If the stain is still there, and if the fabric is colorfast, add a few drops of hydrogen peroxide. Then rinse once more. Launder immediately.

Save on Buttons

One small drop of clear nail polish on your buttons will solidify the threads, keeping them in place. Result? Fewer lost buttons!

Ironing Lace?

The trick to ironing delicate lace is this: using a solution of one-to-one ratio water and sugar, spray on the lace, then iron. The sugar in the solution will stiffen the lace enough to allow for safe ironing.

Scuff Marks

A little nail polish remover works miracles when it comes to removing scuff marks found on shoes. With a dry cloth simply apply the nail polish remover. In most cases, the scuff marks will be gone.

Shoelaces

If knots in your shoelaces are a problem—and they often are a problem—try sprinkling a bit of talcum powder. The crystals in the powder will create the right kind of friction necessary to facilitate untying that stubborn knot.

Keeping Clothes Colorfast

The secret? When doing colors, put in a tablespoon of black pepper. Weird science? Yes, but it works!

Blood Stains

What? The mystery theater dinner party of "Macbeth" went awry? So did mine! Believe it or not, use meat tenderizer and room temperature water to form a paste. It works wonders. The meat tenderizer dissolves most of the blood in the fabric in about an hour. Then rinse in cool water. Launder as usual.

Shoe Smells

Fabric softeners will prevent shoes from smelling. Why? The fabric softener will absorb perspiration as your shoes dry out.

Ink Stain

It isn't just nerds who stain their clothes with pen ink. When that happens to you . . . use hairspray! Hairspray the stain until the fabric is saturated. Then toss in the washing machine. In most cases, the ink stain will wash away.

Taking Prescription Medicines?

Some prescription medications can dye urine the color of deep orange . . . and this can stain undergarments. The same is true of certain antibiotics and drugs used in chemotherapy. The solution is to make a paste of white vinegar and baking soda. Rub into the undergarment, and then launder as usual.

Grease Stains

1. In Yucatán, even Jews and Muslims eat pork—OK, perhaps they don't. But perhaps they should! Oh, who am I to tell people what they should and shouldn't eat? But everyone does, at some point, get grease on their clothes. The solution is not some expensive pre-soak! Simple saturate the stain in liquid dishwashing detergent and cool water. Then wash it in the washing machine as normal.

2. Another remedy? An unsightly grease stain can be removed using baking soda—but you have to act fast. Slowly work the baking soda and soak in warm water afterward.

3. You have two options: work liquid dishwashing detergent into the stain, let rest, and rinse with cool water. Or you can pour talcum powder on the stain and, when dry, brush off. Launder as usual.

Salad Dressings—Oil-Based

Vinaigrettes and other oil-based salad dressings can be readily cleaned by sprinkling cornstarch or baby powder. These substances will absorb most of the oil. Then, after 15 minutes or so, treat with a dishwashing liquid and cool water. NEVER brush in the dishwashing liquid, since this might result in discoloration.

Salad Dressings—Cream-Based

French or Thousand Island dressings can be removed with less work. Immediately soak the stain in cold water for half hour. Then blot. Launder as normal.

No More Ring Around the Collar

It's not you; it's your sweat. A secret for preventing a stain on your shirt or blouse collar is simple: BEFORE you get dressed, use a cotton ball to rub a little bit of rubbing alcohol on the back of your neck. Do this and your perspiration won't leave an oily stain.

Black Clothes are Washed Out?

In this tropical sun, even black clothes fade . . . and when they do the secret to getting them to darken is to add a pot of freshly-brewed coffee to the rinse cycle. The black will be black once more.

Easy Wrinkle Free Sheets

Over-drying your sheets will actually increase wrinkles! The secret? Remove them from the dryer while they are still damp. Then hang them on a clothesline out of direct sunlight. The warm Yucatán breeze will dry them out—

virtually wrinkle-free.

Air Drying, Hangers

Whether it's a pair of jeans or a day blouse, if you make sure you have sturdy hangers, your clothes will thank you. You will also need wardrobe flanges. Place the flanges high on the wall and this will allow for air to circulate freely.

Air Drying, Sheets & Towels

Fold sheets or towels until they are narrow enough to fit through the triangle of the hanger. Both lengths should be even with each other. Alternatively, make sure you hang them on a sturdy clothesline. Think Norman Rockwell—in the tropics!

Air Drying, Air Circulation

If you are drying indoors, use an oscillating fan to circulate the air. If you are drying outdoors, make sure the sun shines on the laundry!

Banish Lint from Washing Machines!

One way of making sure lint doesn't adhere to your laundry in the washing machine is to add a cup of white vinegar along with your detergent. This should prevent lint from clinging to your clothes.

Removing Lint from Dark Jeans

It happens to everyone, doesn't it? Lint on dark jeans! You can wrap duct tape around your hand and, sticky side out; run your hand over the lint. Or you can wash your jeans once again—separately—and add a cup of white vinegar during the rinse cycle.

Clean Dryer Lint Catch

Did you know you will save money if you clean the dryer lint catch once a month? Clean it by running water in your kitchen faucet. This will remove dryer sheet residue that builds up over time, making it a drag on your dryer—and making it use more electricity!

Prevent Jeans from Bleeding

How? Simple! Place your denims in a bucket. Pour three cups white vinegar (or more if necessary). Soak jeans for 15 minutes. Turn your jeans inside out and then launder as usual.

Princess is Parched!

And I am confident you could use a potent potable just about right now. I think I'll have a . . .

GIMLET

2 ounces London dry gin
1 ounce Rose's Lime Juice Cordial

Shake ingredients with ice. Strain into a chilled cocktail glass.

Read "The Short Happy Life of Francis Macomber," a short story by Ernest Hemingway. Do remember that when Francis Macomber's wife, Margot, asks for a gimlet, she is actually asking for both a drink—and a manly husband. In this life, drinks are often metaphors for what we long most in life. But of course you knew that, didn't you?

Drink and read . . . responsibly!

WONDERFUL TIPS FOR YOUR TERRACE AND GARDEN!

Did I tell you?

Has the world changed!
Before there was such a thing as Wikileaks, before that travesty befell the world, one could gossip freely to officials and agents of the U.S. government.

Now?

Today you would have to be a naïf to say anything to anyone who reports to the American government, which apparently has no way of preventing confidential computer servers from being hacked and classified documents from being leaked for the world to read.

I remember decades back when inquiries would arrive, asking if I would help "debrief" officers about what I thought of this Yucatecan politician or that Yucatecan politician. Or worse still, if I knew who was "engaged" in "commercial activities" with Cuba.

Never had time for this sort of nonsense, I'd reply. Do you? Do you have time to figure out what the internal squabbling within, for instance, the Cervera family is all about? Or which entrepreneur is selling hotel toilets to Havana tourism officials?

It's all a game of putting things aside, this silence in the spaces in between. It is the pride of those who refuse to accept that something has gone wrong. After all, something's always wrong. Don't believe me? Darling, it's all there for you to read, in the spaces in between, in the documents Wikileaks released for the world to see.

Gossip to officials or agents of the U.S. government? About what? About the time that, at prodding of Howard Hawks, we agreed to host Cary Grant at our home? Yes, we did invite him, but the timing was never right, although Cary did accept. Or perhaps the time we had lunch with Babe Paley in New York and were gossiping about Nancy Reagan's vulgar décor at the White House? Maybe I could tell them how I was impressed when, visiting Campeche not too long ago with friends from Vienna, I glanced over and took a good look at that stunning

Katy Perry walking to the Puerta del Mar—I'm glad she and Russell Brand divorced; she can do much better than that twit!

This old woman's Most Excellent Adventures . . . Now, *that* would be some hot stuff to Wikileak on Wikileaks or tweet on Twitter or tumble on Tumblr!

Then again, I have more important things to ponder: How do you grow gorgeous roses? How to nurture award-winning heirloom tomatoes! How to find exquisite dark chocolate that approximates the ecstasy of orgasm!

But enough about me and my thrilling Domestic Diva aspirations, let's move on to the matter at hand!

Wonderful Tips for your Terrace and Garden

Banish Mosquitoes

1. Let's face it, tropical environments harbor mosquitoes. This is why you need to tackle the challenge several ways and I don't mean paying someone to fumigate! First remedy: plant basil herbs and tansies (*Tanacetum vulgare*). Tansies are a perennial, herbaceous flowering plant of the aster family. Mosquitoes loathe the scent of basil and tansies and they stay away! (Tansies are also known as Bitter Buttons, Cow Bitter, Mugwort, or Golden Buttons.)

2. Take ½ cup witch hazel, add 10 drops eucalyptus essential oil, vigorously combine by shaking in a spray bottle, and voila! A natural mosquito repellent that you can safely spray on your terrace furniture and potted plants that will drive mosquitoes away!

3. For your garden, try this other recipe: one small onion, and one head of garlic. Chop and mix with four cups water and four teaspoons cayenne pepper. Mix vigorously and then spray on plants—you won't notice the scent, but the mosquitoes will be driven away by it!

4, When enjoying the terrace in the evenings, use incense that contains citrodora and neem—mosquitoes hate the scent, which is actually rather lovely. It's sold under the "Maroma" brand. The better ones are made in Auroville, India. Several shops around town carry Maroma.

5. For pool areas, here's a formula: one ounce concentrated garlic oil and one tablespoon canola oil. Add to one cup water, mix vigorously in a spray bottle, and spray on plants and around the edge of your pool. This scent keeps mosquitoes away and the canola oil will ensure that the spray lingers on the plants, becoming more effective when warmed by the sun!

6. Dress for a mosquito-free lifestyle! Did you know that mosquitoes are naturally attracted to the color dark blue? Banish those jeans when outdoors! Dress in khakis and light-colored garments and mosquitoes are less likely to approach you.

7. When life gives you lemons—and oranges—make a mosquito repellent! Yes, it's true. If you take lemon and orange peels, add one cup water, blend in your blender and then use in a spray bottle, you can safely spray all your plants in the terrace and garden. That citrus scent will keep mosquitoes away.

8. Ever wonder why there are so few, if any, mosquitoes at the beach? The breeze keeps them away! When having a gathering on your terrace, set up fans at ground level, aimed at the floor, so the wind circulates under the tables, protecting everyone's feet and ankles!

9. In your garden, make sure that you plant these five varieties—which exude aromas that drive mosquitoes away: marigolds, catnip, ageratum (also known as flossflowers), citronella, and horsemint (also known as beebalm). These are beautiful plants that are easy to grow. They will make your home a mosquito-free zone!

10. This is a peculiar combination, but one that has worked wonders: mix equal parts eucalyptus oil and fennel seed oil. Pour in a small saucer and leave on your terrace tables. The combination of scents drives mosquitoes far away, creating a mosquito-free zone!

Kill Fire Ants Colonies

1. This works! Boil one gallon water, add ¼ cup liquid detergent, and remove from heat. Pour onto the ant colony. Always make sure you are wearing rubber gloves. Cover your legs and feet. Do this for four consecutive days. It might also kill surrounding grass, so use as appropriate.

2. A more aggressive method involves pouring a quart of cider vinegar inside the ant hill. Do this for four consecutive days. It might also kill surrounding grass, so use as appropriate.

3. The most aggressive method involves pouring a gallon of hot water that has one cup salt mixed in it. Pour this mixture inside the ant hill. Do this for four consecutive days. The salt in the solution may kill nearby plants, which is why this is appropriate for ant colonies near gravel paths or driveways.

Protect Garden Tools

Now that your garden is a mosquito-free zone, it's time to garden! And when you're done gardening, one way to keep your garden tools looking like new is to store them in a small pail—filled with sand! After you wipe clean your garden tools, make sure the metal parts are buried in the sand. This will keep them from rusting.

Protect Gardening Shears

How? In the tropics, it's important to reduce rust . . . and here's where wiping car wax on garden shears will protect them from the elements. Rust-free garden shears have never been easier.

Crystal Clear Vases

Here's the secret to crystal clear vases for all those beautiful flowers and plants you want to showcase on your terrace: pour white vinegar and uncooked rice, and give a swirl. The acidity in the vinegar and the abrasiveness of the rice will clean away the cloudy hard water buildup, leaving you with vases that look brand new!

Nurture your Lawn

One simple way of making your lawn grass grow faster and thrive? Simple! Epsom salts, rich in magnesium and sulfur, will feed your grass and help it flourish! Sprinkle lightly, then water.

The End of Ticks

1. A simple way to remove ticks? Yes, there is. All you have to do is cover the area with petroleum jelly. Fifteen minutes later, the tick will have suffocated. Wipe away with tissue paper.

2. Another simple solution is to moisten a Q-tip with rubbing alcohol. The tick will let go of your pet's skin immediately—just to get away from the sting of the rubbing alcohol!

Keep Bees Away

The easiest solution? If you seem to be a bee-magnet, then consider this: place a sheet of fabric softener in your breast pocket. Bees stay clear! And if you're having guests over, make table decorations with fabric softeners sticking out of them, and you will protect all your guests!

No More Opossums

1. Let's face it, the only cute opossums are in Disney cartoons! And these creatures do wreck havoc on gardens, so the solutions is simply to toss a few moth balls around your flowering plants. For your vegetable garden, plant cucumbers—they hate the scent of cucumbers!

2. These creatures of the night certainly love to scavenge through garbage, don't they? Scavenging through garbage sounds very familiar for anyone who's looked on aghast at the goings on of some of these expat organizations, but enough about the International Women's Club of Mérida! One part ammonia and three parts water, sprayed on both the inside and outside of your garbage cans once a month is usually enough to keep opossums away . . . if it only worked on those fools who busy themselves pontificating from Mérida to the blogosphere!

Neem Soap Spray

Bring one quart water to boil. Remove from heat. Add neem soap shavings . . . and you have a natural insect repellent that you can spray on flowering plants around your terrace. Flies and other insects will steer clear!

Ant-Free Patio Parties

Here's an insurance policy for your next garden party: one tablespoon peppermint essential oil and one quart water. Mix. Spray on floor, furniture, tables, seats, and window sills a couple of hours before you begin to set up. The peppermint oil scent will keep ants away—and the entire area will smell fresh and inviting!

The End of the Ant Problem

Ants invading your garden? The solution is simple: pour cornmeal where they are. The ants will eat the cornmeal, but they aren't able to digest it, and they soon die out. This is an old Maya remedy for doing away with ant invasions. Now you know!

Keep Ants Away from Your Terrace

Grind up orange peels and mix with one cup of water. Pour solution into a spray bottle. Spray around your terrace and ants will stay away!

Keep Ants Away from Your Outdoor Grill Area

Remember chalk from your school days? Take white chalk and draw a perimeter around your terrace. Ants will mistake the chalk for ash, presume they are about to enter a burned out fire zone, and immediately make an about face!

Keep Ants Away from Your Kitchen Windows and Counter

Combine one cup water and one tablespoon cinnamon. Mix vigorously and spray. Ants loathe the smell of cinnamon and stay away.

Adios Cucarachas!

1. It's possible to empower you Killer Within . . . by killing roaches—without poison. How? Equal parts sugar and baking powder. Mix well and sprinkle where you've seen roaches. Did you know that roaches die soon after eating baking powder? Now you do!

2. Another holistic solution to killing roaches? Especially in this town? Pour leftover wine in a small bowl and leave out where you've seen the roaches. They will be drawn to the wine, but become drunk, fall in, and drown.

3. This method works splendidly for terraces and patios: equal parts plaster of Paris and cornstarch sprinkled where you've seen the roaches. They will come for the cornstarch but the plaster of Paris will poison them once consumed.

Kill Grasshoppers!

Did you know that tomato leaves are poisonous? Well, you know now! And what do they kill most effectively? Grasshoppers and crickets! Crush tomato leaves and soak in water overnight. Strain into spray bottle. Spray grasshoppers! Make sure you do not spray food bearing plants!

Kill Aphids

Boil one cup water and add basil leaves. When cool, strain. Add one teaspoon liquid dishwashing detergent. Spray on aphids. The basil will kill them and the dishwashing detergent will make sure the solution does not wash off before the aphids are dead.

No More Garden Spiders!

How? Why, it's Easy, Breezy! Bring four cups water to a boil. Add one cup orange or lemon peels. Add half an onion. Remove from heat. When cool, spray on your garden plants. The citrus oil and onion scent will keep spiders off your plants!

Keep Birds Away from Your Fruit Trees

How? Why simple! Cut strips of aluminum foils and hang among your fruit trees. Birds will go right for the shining aluminum, strike, become startled and fly off!

Boiling Eggs?

Did you know that when you boil eggs, calcium leaches into the water . . . and that this calcium-rich water works wonders for flowering plants! Once it cools down, water your plants with this water for more abundant flowers!

Weeds No More!

The best time to weed your garden is always late afternoon, usually after 5 PM. Why? In the tropics, the most intense heat dissipates between 5 PM and 6 PM. By coincidence, it's easier to weed after an afternoon shower, which usually occurs between 2 PM and 4 PM.

Make Weeds Feel Unwelcome!

To reduce weeds, try this: plant devil's ivy, winter creeper or lily-of-the-valley. (The scientific name for Devil's ivy is *Epipremnum aureum*. I mention this because it is commonly mislabeled as *Philodendron* in most plant shops!) These plants stake their ground, inhibiting invasive weeds!

Natural Fertilizer

Grass trimmings, combined with dried banana peels, make for a wonderful, economical fertilizer. Simply distribute among the stems of garden plants.

Compost Time!

In the tropics there are no excuses for NOT having a compost—and if you have no idea where to start, here's an invaluable resource on composing for those readers living in Yucatán: Nancy Walker Olvera. Look her up on Facebook!

(https://www.facebook.com/nancy.walkerolvera)

Keeping Garden Plants Healthy

Oh, did I mention that it's imperative to have a bucket with a solution of ¼ cup bleach to one gallon water nearby? It's important to disinfect pruning shears, since this will reduce the chance of your spreading disease from one plant to the next.

Leave Town Often?

If you're the kind to say *vámonos*—"let's go"—and then take off for a week or so, then you simply have to place sponges at the bottom of your plants next time you re-pot them? Why? Because the sponge will absorb extra moisture—and your potted plants will stay hydrated while you're off having fun.

Prevent Flowers from Wilting

In the tropics, cut flowers wilt very quickly, but here's a trick I've found to be true. When you arrange fresh-cut flowers, add half a can of soda—preferably a clear one, such as 7-Up. The sugars will nourish your flowers and the carbonation will inhibit bacteria from attacking the stems as quickly!

Extend the Life of Flowers

Another way of extending the life of cut flowers? Try this remedy: a shot of gin or vodka or tequila poured into a vase filled with fresh flowers will extend the life of your beautiful arrangement. The secret? The alcohol will kill bacteria that attack the stem of cut flowers and the sugars in liquor will feed the cut flowers. Now you know.

Tea Time!

Did I tell you that if you mix whatever tea (or leftover coffee) you have on hand, you can use to water your potted plants? Why spend money on fertilizers?

Fertilize Your Plants Some More!

Who needs to purchase anything from Home Depot when you already have wonderful sources of potassium and nitrogen for your plants! Yes, put those banana peels in the sun to dry them out, then combine with coffee grinds . . . and what do you have? A wonderful fertilizer to mix into your plants' soil!

Keep Flies Away from Your Terrace

Having friends over for lunch? Keep flies away by hanging three or four CLEAR PLASTIC bags filled with water from the ceiling! What? Yes! Rays of light will create prisms that flies find disorienting—and they stay clear of the area!

Keep Raccoons Away

In the States, it's bears and in the tropics it's raccoons—so how do you protect your garbage cans from being ransacked by raccoons? Believe it or not, scatter *dog hair* around your garbage cans! Raccoons will think you have raccoon-killing canines nearby! It's that simple. Any pet grooming place in town has dog hair to give away for free!

Easy After Party Cleaning Up

If you squeeze the juice of one lime into a bowl with a little Comet (or other similar cleaning product), you have a super cleaner for your grilling area—that easily dissolves grease and grime!

Cleaning Your Hands

Cucumber peels will neutralize and dissolve greasy residues on your hands, as well as dirt, so this is a wonderful natural solution. Simply have a bowl with cucumber peels soaking in it, dip your fingers, and wipe your hands. Then wash your hands as usual.

Keep Weeds to a Minimum

How? Wet old newspapers and layer around your garden. Cover with mulch or potting soil. The newsprint will create a natural barrier as it decays, minimizing weeds from sprouting!

"White Fly" Invasion

It came from Florida, or so the rumor is! Who knows, but wherever they came from, white flies—comprising only the family *Aleyrodidae*—are now a problem. Fortunately, the solution is simple: plant mint and nasturtiums in your garden. They hate these plants and will fly elsewhere!

Keep Mice Away!

Here's the recipe: two tablespoons castor oil, five tablespoons dishwashing detergent, one tablespoon Tabasco sauce, one minced garlic clove, and one quart water. Mix ingredients and pour around where the mice hide in your garden and terrace areas.

Keep Moles Away!

Here's the recipe: ½ cup liquid detergent, one tablespoon Tabasco sauce, and one gallon water. Mix ingredients and pour around where the moles have been spotted in your garden and terrace.

Keep Small Mammals Away!

An effective poison for small mammals—mice, rats, moles—is to combine equal parts cornflower and powder cement. Use raisins or peanut butter as bait. The rodents will eat the cornflower and cement, and then seek out water to quench their thirst. The water will react with the cement, effectively killing the animal quickly.

No More Silverfish!

An effective trap can be prepared by combining equal parts flour and Borax. Place in small holders (cupcake foil works well). Place where the silverfish have been spotted. The flour will attract them and the Borax will kill them.

Satchels to Repel Spiders, Ants & Silverfish

1. Make sachets to leave on bookshelves and in drawers to keep these pests away. What do you put inside the sachets? Rosemary, lavender buds, and whole cloves.

2. Make sachets to leave on bookshelves and in drawers to keep these pests away. What do you put inside the sachets? Lavender buds, one piece of cinnamon stick, and whole cloves.

The End of Slugs!

After a party, how many bottles of Corona or Bohemia beer are left all over the place? I'll bet that some are not completely empty. Use that leftover beer to rid yourself of slugs! How? Pour the beer into a shallow bowl—an aluminum pie pan is perfect—and leave it on the sidewalk. The slugs love beer, make their way to the shallow bowl, become intoxicated, and drown!

I'm Looking Over . . . Clover!

Not only is clover a wonderful green covering, but it also provides necessary nutrients to the roots of almost all your garden plants, saving you a fortune on fertilizers.

Garlic in your Garden

Grow garlic on the edge of your garden and beetles will never invade your garden!

Fresh Birdbath

Who doesn't want lovely birds around their garden? To attract them, try this: pour multi-colored marbles into your birdbath. Those dazzling colors, reflected in the water, will attract birds.

A Cleaner Birdbath

In this climate, algae grow wild! Here's a secret: empty your birdbath and scrub clean with a mixture of lime juice and baking soda. When clean, refill with water—only this time, add lavender flowers. This is a trick that French guests have taught me over the years: lavender inhibits algae!

Feed Your Garden Plants!

On the cheap—How? Easy, Breezy! Simply save the water in which you boil pasta or potatoes. Garden plants thrive on starched water . . . no need to spend a fortune on expensive potting fertilizers!

Re-Pot Properly

How? In the tropics, it's good to place used coffee filters—or even moistened newsprint—in the bottom of pots before you re-pot? Why? Moisture retention, silly!

Exuberant Ferns

Ferns are such a treat in the tropics. So gorgeous! And ferns thrive, flourish, and will enrich your life if you dry out banana peels and then bury them in the soil. Banana peels are wonderful fertilizers for ferns of every variety. (It's the potassium in banana peels!)

Store Seeds

Where? In the freezer, of course! Many seeds need a period of hibernation, and there's no better way to simulate winter than wrapping seeds in paper towels, putting them in plastic zip bags, and storing in the freezer until you are ready for them.

Dust Mites Be Gone!

One time-tested method for getting rid of dust mites is cinnamon bark oil. Mix equal part water and cinnamon bark oil. Spray on carpets and bedding. They will soon be a thing of the past.

Kill Flea Eggs—Naturally!

Fleas have a three day reproduction cycle. That means that for nine days you have to engage this remedy: Salt your carpet and area rugs every day, vacuuming every third day. Every time you vacuum, empty the bag—otherwise, live fleas will crawl right out of the vacuum bag.

Fake Wasps Out!

Did you know that wasps are territorial? Most species will not build nests within 200 yards of rivals' next. For a few dollars, you can buy a fake wasp nest to hang in strategic places—and the wasps will be off to nest elsewhere!

Keep Spiders from Entering Your Windows

How? That's Easy, Breezy! Simply mix equal parts lemon or lime juice and water. Spay on windowsills. It works because spiders loathe citrus scents and will not venture into your home through the windows!

Keep Mosquitoes from Entering Your Windows

Oh, did I tell you? Mosquitoes detest catnip. Window boxes that grow catnip among the flowers will naturally deter mosquitoes from approaching your home.

Keep Flies from Entering Your Windows

A kitchen can minimize the arrival of flies if you grow basil in your window sills. Flies are averse to the scent of basil and will not fly near it.

Removing Sap from Your Hands

How? Well, now that you've asked, here's the remedy: butter. Rub butter into the sap and then wash your hands, wrists, forearms or elbows—and the sap will be history.

Blooming Roses

Believe me when I tell you that fat drippings are the answer. . . whether you are cooking up bacon, or chicken or a roast. One half cup drippings mixed with half cup water are what you need for rose bushes. Then sit back and watch the roses bloom! Gorgeous!

Egg Shells to the Rescue

If you have a vegetable or herb garden, by simply spreading crushed egg shells around the base of the stems you will keep slugs and snails away. They are averse to navigating egg shells. Odd, but true.

Princess is Parched!

And I am confident you could use a potent potable just about right now. I think I'll have a . . .

CLASSIC DAIQUIRI

2 ounces white rum
1 teaspoon grapefruit juice
1 teaspoon maraschino liqueur
½ ounce fresh lime juice

Crush ice. In a shaker, put crushed ice, and add ingredients. Shake well. Pour into a chilled cocktail glass.

Read *Islands in the Stream* by Ernest Hemingway. Who could forget this description of a daiquiri: "This frozen daiquiri, so well beaten as it is, looks like the sea where the wave falls away from the bow of a ship when she is doing thirty knots. How do you think frozen daiquiris would be if they were phosphorescent?" But of course you knew that, didn't you?

Drink and read . . . responsibly!

WONDERFUL TIPS FOR REMOVING STAINS!

Did I tell you?

A while back I journeyed to an event in Centro. It was one of those rare outings for me, given my preference for the more leisurely life in the country.

Darling, I have to tell you, was I aghast!

After making the effort of attending this event, the hostess—who looked like that disheveled character Mrs. Roper on the old sitcom, "Three's Company"—was holding court. With half a bottle of wine splashing around in a goblet, that old drunk staggered around her over-the-top excess of a home. Truly a sad sight; I have never returned.

I mention this because, as I saw in my friends Ernest Hemingway and Truman Capote, alcoholism is a disease that kills. And although I offer some of my favorite cocktails in this book, this in no way is an endorsement of drinking in anything but moderation.

A couple of decades back, a good friend, who lived in Bloomfield Hills, Michigan during the summer but faithfully traveled to Mérida each winter, also succumbed to that disease. Before she had to return to Michigan permanently, we loved to socialize.

She and I would spend lovely afternoons together. I would travel to her place, not far from Parque de las Américas, or she would come visit us out here. She was a wonderful friend, but I have to confess that in her later years, as alcoholism possessed her completely, we kept our distance because of her eccentric and erratic behavior.

Imagine my surprise, for instance, when I arrived for a visit to find that the guest bedroom had been wallpapered with photographs of Jacqueline Kennedy mourning at JFK's funeral taken from LIFE magazine. You know the photograph, the black-and-white one in which Mrs. Kennedy has that stricken expression on her face. She wears a veil. All four walls were covered in this image. Framed black-and-white photographs of zebras hung against this travesty! (It upset my husband greatly, especially since his family was close to the Bouvier family.) Empty bottles of wine and gin were strewn all about her home.

Nutty things like that made me wonder about the power of that disease. Sanity requires stamina few can muster.

But enough about me and my pontifications, let's move on to the matter at hand!

Wonderful Tips for Removing Stains

Gentle Reminder:

Test the color steadfastness of the fabric before using any stain removal remedy.

Always treat stains as soon as they occur in order to prevent them from setting. If that happens, stains become more difficult or impossible to remove.

To test a fabric or other material (such as a carpet or rug), first apply a few drops of the solution, such as hydrogen peroxide, in an inconspicuous area on the fabric. Please make sure the color does not fade or become discolored.

Do not use the solution to remove any stain on any fabric if the color fades, becomes discolored or is not colorfast.

Antique Linens

1. Try at your own risk! Antique linens, lace, and tablecloths often yellow because they have been improperly stored—which is often! The first method is to try to identify the source of the stain—food, mildew, yellowing from heat or age? The gentlest approach is to soak in tepid water and to use a mild detergent. Rinse and let it air dry. If the stain is still there, you may have to try more aggressive methods, listed below.

2. Try at your own risk! Saturate the stained fabric in a solution of one part water and one part white vinegar. Be mindful that vinegar will weaken lace and delicate fabrics. Be prudent in the time you allow the fabric to sit in this solution before rinsing and air drying.

3. Try at your own risk! If the stain is still there, the most aggressive remedy is to use one quart water, adding one tablespoon lemon juice. Use an eyedropper to test the fabric's ability to endure the acidity of the lemon. If it is safe, then apply a couple of drops, rinse in the solution, and let it dry in the sun. This should "bleach" away the stain.

Berries

Soak fabric in one cup white vinegar and one cup whole milk for at least 6 hours. Then launder as usual.

Blood

Immediately pour club soda or hydrogen peroxide on the stain. If it has dried, make a paste from club soda and baking soda or cornstarch. Apply to the stain. When dry, brush. Launder as usual.

Chocolate Stains

Oh, this is a delicious problem to have! Chocolate! Bury me in chocolate and I will only be too happy. But if a chocolate stain has occurred in this lifetime, try this remedy: mix a gentle liquid detergent or hand soap with hydrogen peroxide. Saturate the stain for 15 minutes. Then wash immediately. If the chocolate stain is on a sofa or pillow, blot the solution and keep blotting with a damp cloth until you remove the detergent and hydrogen peroxide completely. Of course you have already checked to see if the fabrics are colorfast, right?

Coffee

If the fabric is color-safe, stretch the garment over a bowl in the kitchen sink or bathtub. Cover the stain with salt, then pour a cup of boiling water over it.

Launder as usual.

Cooking Oil

Shampoo does the trick. Saturate the stain and let sit for half an hour. Rinse in cool water. Launder as usual.

Deodorants

Soak fabric in white vinegar for 20 minutes, then rinse in cool water. If necessary, repeat. Launder as usual.

Gasoline

How did you get this on your clothes? No matter. There are two ways to remove the stain and smell. First, pour Coca-Cola and baking soda on the stain, letting it saturate the fabric. Let it soak overnight. The next morning, rinse in cold water. If this hasn't done the job, gently apply baby oil to the stained area. Launder as usual.

Grass Stains

1. The surest way to remove grass stains is by mixing 1/8 cup hydrogen peroxide with two to three drops of ammonia and—wearing rubber gloves—rub it on the stain. Launder as usual!

2. Another trick is to scrub toothpaste into the stain with an old toothbrush. Launder as usual.

3. Another time-tested remedy is saturating the stain with laundry detergent and the juice of half a lemon. Gently scrub with a toothbrush. Launder as usual.

4. A final solution: forget those expensive stain removers! Simply rub a little agave sweetener or corn syrup into the fabric and wash as you normally do.

Gum

Warm half a cup of vinegar and, using a toothbrush, saturate the gum. Then slowly brush it out. It should work on most fabrics. Another method is to place the garment in the freezer—then scrape off the frozen gum with a dull knife.

Ink

This is a common problem, isn't it? This is especially the case in warm climates where ink runs more freely. There are two solutions. The most successful one is to cut an onion and rub it into the stain. Add a few drops of lime juice. Launder. The other solution is to pour hydrogen peroxide on the stain until it almost vanishes. Launder as usual.

Ketchup

This is straightforward: a little hydrogen peroxide works wonders. Let it has saturated the fabric for a few minutes. Launder as usual.

Lipstick

1. Oh, yes, this is a common stain, isn't it? Especially in the tropics, where Latin Lovers abound . . . But more about that later! Lipstick can be easily removed by rubbing petroleum jelly into the stain. Launder as normal.

2. Another remedy is to blot the lipstick stain with rubbing alcohol. Blot using a paper towel and keep applying alcohol.

3. Another time-tested method is to saturate the lipstick stain with hairspray. Then let sit for about 15 minutes and rinse with warm water.

Mustard

A little hydrogen peroxide works wonders. After saturating the fabric for a few minutes with hydrogen peroxide, launder as usual.

Perspiration

There are two ways of treating perspiration stains: 1) Saturate with lime juice, then pour hydrogen peroxide. Launder as usual. 2) Pulverize four or five regular aspirin tablets, mix in ½ cup warm water and blot the stain. Launder as usual.

Rust

Blot the rust stain with lime juice and warm water. Pour salt. Let it sit for an hour. Launder as usual.

Salsa

Whether you made it yourself or (dare I say it, darling?) you bought it at Costco, the solution is the same: a little hydrogen peroxide works wonders. After it has saturated the fabric for a few minutes, launder as usual.

Shoe Polish

For white fabrics, just pour alcohol and rub before laundering as normal. For colorfast fabrics, dilute the alcohol (one part alcohol to two parts water), soak stain, and then launder as usual.

Tobacco

There are two methods: 1) pour hydrogen peroxide on the spot, and then launder as usual; 2) moisten stain and saturate with dishwashing detergent, and then launder as usual.

Wine

1. Pour salt on the stain. Then pour hydrogen peroxide. Launder as usual.
2. Another solution is to pour hydrogen peroxide and baking soda. Launder as usual.

Removing Grape Juice Stains

Blot the stain with lemon juice. Spray a mixture of equal parts white vinegar and water. Keep blotting until stain is gone. Launder immediately.

Coffee Stain

Few things clean coffee stains better than white vinegar! Simply blot the stain with white vinegar and launder as soon as possible.

Linoleum

Stains on linoleum surfaces can be removed using bleach and then pouring baking soda on the stain. Let it set, then rinse thoroughly with water.

Bathtub Stains

Whether the tub is antique or contemporary, if it's a metal tub then it requires a mixture of baking soda and vinegar. Mix the paste until it is watery. Brush it into the stain. Let it dry and then rinse the tub.

Cleaner Car for Road Trips,

1. Hitting the road to Campeche or Cancún? Whichever direction you head out in, wipe a light coat of vegetable oil on the grill of your car and polish your windshield with car wax. Have I gone mad? Of course not! But in the tropics, road trips mean lots of splattered bugs . . . and the vegetable oil and car wax will create a natural barrier. Upon arrival at your destination, a quick hosing down will be sufficient to wash away all the dead bugs!
2. Club soda in a spray bottle, with a few drops of hand washing soap, is all you need to wipe away bug guts and bird droppings on other parts of your car. It's that Easy, Breezy!

Tire Marks

1. No need to tell you that with this "polished cement" madness . . . there are consequences! How many driveways now have cement floors, polished or otherwise, with tire stains? The first course of action is laundry detergent and warm water—with a strong brush!

2. If this doesn't work, the it's time for trisodium phosphate (TSP), which is *Fosfato trisódico* in Spanish, and is available at most hardware stores. Be mindful that this is a corrosive agent, so it might not be suitable for polished cement surfaces—and certainly not for exposed skin! Always wear rubber gloves. Scrub, then hose down thoroughly. If the stain is still there, avail yourself to the third option, below.

3. The last resort is to rent a professional pressure washer. When you rent one, be sure to get a model that is capable of 3,000 pounds of pressure per square inch. If this doesn't do the trick, any other method will most likely involve removing the finish off your concrete.

Remove Tea Stains from Porcelain

Fill cup or saucer with warm water. Pour table salt and swirl. Let stand half an hour. Rinse in warm water. Repeat if necessary.

Remove Sticker Residue from Leather

What kind of glue do they use on stickers? I don't know, but I do know they should know better than to put a sticker label on leather! But they do that often enough, don't they. To remove the sticky residue, use a cotton ball and baby oil. In soft circular motions rub the residue. When the residue is soft, use white vinegar and a clean cloth to wipe the baby oil. Dry the area with another soft, lint-free cloth.

Princess is Parched!

And I am confident you could use a potent potable just about right now. I think I'll have a . . .

CAMPARI & GIN

2 ounces London dry gin
1 ounce Campari

Pour ingredients over ice in a chilled highball glass.

Read *True at First Light* by Ernest Hemingway. This sentence always comes to mind when I crave a Campari & Gin: "I'll take Campari with just a little gin." Yes, 1 ounce Campari and 2 ounces gin! But of course you knew that, didn't you?

Drink and read . . . responsibly!

WONDERFUL TIPS FOR ENTERTAINING!

Did I tell you?

After a period of melancholy after my husband died, I resolved to break out of my self-imposed isolation. Life is for the living. We had discussed this, both of us expressing that whatever came our way, the one left to carry on would forge ahead and enjoy life.

Of course, that's always easier said than done. *Look for the girl with the broken smile . . .*

Darling, it's always easier to forge ahead and enjoy life's beauty—with an unbroken heart!

It was then, that, with the encouragement of friends and family, I resolved to start dining out. There really are wonderful restaurants in Mérida. I'm not going to enumerate which is the best and why, but I do have to recognize just one place I adore.

Yes, Nectar remains my favorite. Roberto Solis continues to amaze. The first time I was there I enjoyed duck chimichanga and the Vietnamese tacos. These dishes sealed the deal for me. I made it a point to visit when Rene Redzepi was there in January 2011. It was a lovely experience. I also have to mention that Caroline Aebi at Le Café De Bruxelles is a gorgeous young woman making the most splendid waffles in Mexico! I'm still on the fence trying to decide which *Puertas Cerradas*, or "Closed Doors," event I have enjoyed the best, but I'll make up my mind soon enough!

Of course everyone of my friends has a favorite dive they rave over, and truth be told, there are wonderful places that serve scrumptious meals. I'm amazed by the *flor de calabaza* at Platos Rotos, or the simple tacos at La Lupita in Santiago market.

But, then again, there's something to be said for formal, sit-down meals when entertaining at home. I remember once I cried when the candles for a dinner party burned too quickly, dripping wax all over my table setting. I was embarrassed. These were dear friends I had wanted to impress.

Well, as my departed husband used to say, "Worse things happen at sea."

Yes, they do.

But enough about me and my wax-soaked table setting, let's move on to the matter at hand!

Wonderful Tips for Entertaining

An Ideal Kitchen for the Tropics

1. Kitchen scissors, I am convinced, was the only set of tools in the home of Mrs. Indiana Jones. It had to be! From cutting a whole raw chicken to an artisanal pizza, there are more uses for kitchen scissors than you can imagine. Invest in a pair of scissors!

2. Garlic press! Get in the habit of adding more garlic to your food. This is a splendid way of improving your health while enlivening your meals!

3. Vegetable peelers are great not only for carrots, but they are ideal for curls of chocolate and parmesan cheese! I'm surprised when a tropical kitchen doesn't have one!

4. Immersion blenders are key to healthier living, whether it is to make a shake or blend more vegetables in your soups. They are wonderful for making cauliflower soups and pureeing mash potatoes.

5. Bamboo steamer? In the tropics, with so many great vegetables? From tamales to steaming squash, nothing is more indispensable!

6. Along with the bamboo steamer, parchment paper is a must! What better way to steam fish, or line a pan when making chocolate brownies?

7. The mandolin is ideal for slicing vegetables, especially if you make your own potato chips, fennel salads or are cooking up all manner of squash and eggplant dishes! Get one—and use it safely!

8. A salad spinner is indispensable, especially since in the tropics it is vital to wash greens and vegetables before assembling salads. Yes, bacteria thrive in warmer climes!

9. A soda maker is a must if you are to enjoy properly all the wonderful seasonal fruit that are harvested year round. Make extraordinary *aguas frescas* that will blow your guests away for pennies by using whatever fruit is in season and a little lemon juice to make something special.

10. A panini press is a must for warming up—or toasting—sandwiches. Here in the Yucatán, with so many Cuban residents, there's nothing like Medianoche Cuban sandwich . . . accompanied by a *café con leche*!

Gracious Hosting

1. If you are hosting visitors overnight, make sure the guest bedroom is comfortable. Open the windows to let the air circulate. Run a fan to freshen up the air, turn the thermostat to a comfortable temperature a few hours before they arrive, and make sure that the windows can be easily opened.

2. On the bedside table, make sure they have an alarm clock and there is an adequate reading lamp. Even if they have a Kindle or the latest tablet, everyone still needs a good bedside lamp. If you leave reading material that might be of interest, that'd be very gracious of you.

3. Make sure they have adequate space in the closet—including hangers—and at least two empty drawers in the dressers.

4. Leave them some snacks. I always leave a jar of home-made cookies, along with a bowl of fruit, with small plates and knives. A small fridge might be appropriate, which is always easier than leaving bottled water and a bucket of ice! Think of the amenities you enjoyed most the last time you were at a hotel. Do the same—but without the alcohol! You don't want houseguests drinking in bed! They should be drinking with you!

5. Make sure the guest bathroom is spotless and that you leave out enough fresh towels, linens, and toilet tissue for them. Leaving new toothbrushes and personal size toothpaste is a lovely touch. Don't forget an air freshener—guests feel awkward asking for it after the fact! And there's nothing wrong with having an aromatic candle to scent the room prior to their arrival or fresh flowers from your garden!

6. Basket of goodies is always fun, by which I mean local magazines (*Explore Yucatán*), a travel book (Moon publications are terrific!) and a list of recommendations (include your favorites, such as going to Ek Balam or Mayapán), and small toiletries—Neem Products at Café Orgánico or Ki' Xocolatl shampoo, soap, and other spa products.

7. Always inquire about any dietary restrictions your guests may have—and accommodate them. This means leaving both a list of suggested meals that you would like to share with them, along with an itinerary of "must see" places in town or around Mérida. This, of course, includes a list of favorite restaurants, cafes, and cultural venues that you yourself enjoy!

A Welcome Treat

A splendid way to welcome guests—and one that is frugal—is a tropical fruit and sorbet bar. What's in season? Stock up on those rather than buying strawberries, grapes, and kiwis from Costco! And to entice your guests into trying "exotic" fruit—*guanabana, zapote*—pick up sorbets from Sorbetería Colón. You won't believe the number of times that someone tries *mamey* sorbet—and then can't wait to try the *mamey* fruit! "For a fruit that looks like a football, it's wonderful!" I've been told. Really?

A Hot Dog Bar

Serve up some American-style hot dogs and buns, with every kind of "American" topping, from onions to relish, mustard and ketchup, to chili and cheese. An American Night is a fun, simple way to give your guests a lovely, low-key break from feeling the need to have Mexican or Yucatecan cuisine for every meal while they're visiting.

A Picnic Lunch for the Ruins

It is charming to pack a picnic basket or cooler for trips to the ruins. Our favorites used to be Ek Balam and Mayapán, and we always packed bottled water, fresh fruit, and healthy meals. This included granola or energy bars, along with a simple casserole. They were always a hit, and prevented our guests from resorting to either a tourist trap restaurant—or foraging at an Oxxo or Pemex station for junk food!

Flavored Fruit Waters

A blender, bottled water, and seasonal fruit, that's all you need to have *aguas* on hand—water that's flavored in seasonal fruit!

Plan for Siestas!

In the tropics, the midday heat exhausts the human organism! Plan accordingly, giving your guests time to return, rest, linger a while in the pool, and take a siesta before the evening's activities begin. Our rule of thumb was always to advise everyone return by three and that nothing would start before six. Of course, there was always something out in the kitchen for guests to snack on between reading, napping, and lounging poolside.

Entertainment Checklist

Whenever you are hosting an event, here is a mandatory checklist that you have to go through to make sure that almost everything is covered. This way, your event will be an Easy, Breezy affair!

FOR COCKTAIL HOUR

- Assortment of cheeses
- Assortment of crackers
- Cheese knives
- Cheese twists
- Crudités
- Cocktail glasses (lowball and martini)
- Flowers (for display)
- Gin
- Grapes, sliced apples, or pears
- Hummus
- Lemonade (unsweetened)
- Lemons
- Limes
- Mezcal
- Mixed nuts
- Napkins (if using paper, allow for 2 for each guest)
- Olives (pits in for eating, stuffed for martinis)
- Platters
- Playlist (if nothing else, sign up for Pandora and have an appropriate playlist)
- Salami
- Seasonal tropical fruit
- Small canapé plates
- Soda
- Teas, including sorrel (unsweetened)

- Tequila
- Tonic (1 bottle for every 3 guests)
- Toothpicks
- Tortillas (warm, handmade)
- Vodka
- Water glass (1 for every guest)
- Wine (1 bottle for every 2-3 guests)
- Wine glass (1 for every guest)

FOR DINNER

- Candles
- Centerpiece
- Napkins
- Place cards (optional)
- Tablecloth

FOR SERVING

- Breadboard or basket
- Bread plates
- Decanter
- Dessert plates
- Dinner plates
- Salad plates
- Serving platters
- Silverware
- Steak knives (if applicable)
- Water goblets
- Water pitcher
- Wine coasters
- Wine glasses

Better Candles

If you store candles in the freezer a few hours before your dinner party, they will burn far more slowly and reduce how much wax they drip. Problem solved, for dinner parties in the warm tropics!

Candle Wax

Melted candle wax on cloth can be readily removed if you place the item in the freezer for a couple of hours. It's a breeze to scrap off excess wax now that it's frozen. Any wax stain can then be removed by placing a piece of paper and ironing—the heat will transfer the wax to the paper!

Make Candles Dripless

Reduce candle wax with this time-proven method: place your candles in a shallow pan and fill with enough water to cover the candles. Add two tablespoons of salt per candle. Let the candles soak for three or four hours in the salt water. Remove, dry, and store in the freezer for a few hours. Do this two days before your party. The salt-fortified candles will drip far less!

Exquisite China and Glassware

Before the table is set, run all your crystal and china through the rinse cycle in your dishwasher—with lemon juice instead of detergent, provided your dishes and glassware are dishwasher-safe. The result will be absolutely sparkling!

Piñata Favors

Believe it or not, score major host or hostess points by simply hanging a traditional seven-starred piñata as décor and preparing lovely candied treats for your guests to take home. Place the takeaway bags of goodies on each guest's dinner plate. If Gramercy Tavern in New York sends guests home with a breakfast muffin, why can't you send your guests with a piñata-inspired bag of treats by which to remember the evening?

Stuck Wine Bottle Cork?

No more! It can happen to the best of us, a stuck cork bottle making it impossible to uncork. The secret? Simply soak a cloth napkin in hot water and wrap around the wine bottle's neck. The warmth will make the glass expand slightly, making it easier to dislodge the stubborn cork.

Rich Vietnamese Style Coffee

For some reason, the tropics make everyone crave sweets! Here is a perennial favorite that I learned when we spent three weeks in Saigon, or Ho Chi Minh City, depending on your political preference. Equal parts condensed milk and espresso. Sublime! And it can be poured over ice for an instant delight that is better than anything Starbucks offers!

Flavored Coffee on Demand!

One wonderful way to end the evening is to offer guests flavored coffee—without breaking the bank stocking up on different varieties. How? Before you individually brew cups of coffee, add dried orange peel, vanilla extract or cinnamon to flavor coffee per that person's request. A ¼ teaspoon suffices for most flavorings, or three drops of vanilla extract.

Champagne's Bubbly Joy

Warm weather makes champagne go flat faster. I'll bet you knew that! But what you probably didn't know is that if you toss two or three raisins in the champagne bottle, the remaining carbon dioxide will cling to the raisins, and then be released as bubbles!

Obedient Plastic Wrap

How do you keep plastic wrap from clinging to itself—which always happens when you're in a hurry and you end up wasting so much? Simple: place the plastic wrap in the refrigerator for a couple of hours before you intend to use it. When cold, plastic wrap is less likely to cling to itself.

Obedient Rolling Pin

What holds true for plastic wrap, holds true for rolling pins! Place your rolling pin in the freezer an hour or so before you need it. Dough is less likely to stick to a cold pin than one at room temperature!

Barbecue Grill Insect Repellent

If you pour some beer into jars and place these strategically around the perimeter of your grilling areas, flying insects will be more drawn to the savory beer than your grilled feast, or your guests. What an Easy, Breezy insect repellent for outdoor grilling!

Serving Cheese

Straight from the refrigerator is not the best way of serving cheese! It's tempting to do so in the tropics, but the best flavor is always found when cheese is allowed to rest for about half an hour. This allows the cheese to become more fragrant and the textures more agreeable to the palate!

Warmer Rolls

Want to keep dinner rolls warmer? Simple! Place a ceramic tile in the oven—ceramics soak up heat. Then place the ceramic tile at the bottom of the dinner roll basket. The tile will keep the dinner rolls warmer for your guests to enjoy.

Crystal Clear Ice Cubes

The secret to gorgeous ice cubes? Now that you've asked, here's the answer: *Boil* the water first, let cool, then pour into ice cube trays and place in the freezer. You will have crystal clear ice cubes!

Better Hors D'oeuvres

If you dampen slightly a few paper towels and careful place over your trays of hors d'oeuvres, you'll make sure they don't dry out, since there's a tendency for fillings to dry out in warmer climates!

Freshen Your Hands

Garlic? Onion? If you simply rub a tablespoon of mouthwash into your palms and fingers, then rinse. These strong scents will be gone.

Airy Pancakes and Cupcakes

To make pancakes—that you can saturate with Canadian maple syrup and fresh fruit—or the lightest cupcakes in the world, try this simple tip: substitute club soda for water when preparing the mix!

Sweeten Up a Mango, Pronto!

So many mango varietals in the tropics! But once in a while one turns out acidic. Simple solution: place the mango in tepid—not hot!—water for about ten minutes. The heat will accelerate the process of starches turning into sugar . . . and your mango will be sweeter than before!

Radiant Radishes

After removing stems, washing, and cleaning, let your radishes soak in a bowl of cool water. They will become succulent beyond belief!

Red Onions to Delight

How? It's Easy, Breezy: slice the onion however way you want, then squeeze one sour orange (Valencia orange, or *naranja agria*). The sour orange will remove the "rawness" from the red onion while imparting a divine taste!

Shelling Nuts

Did you know that if you freeze walnuts, pistachios, and pecans first, when you then remove them from the freezer and warm up to room temperature it's far easier to shell them? Now you do, darling!

Grating Soft Cheese

How hot does it get in tropics? If you have to ask . . . But mindful of this, remember that when grating soft cheeses, put them in the freezer for five minutes. This will harden them enough to make for easier grating!

Fresher Poultry and Meats

Should you find yourself in the supermarket and shopping for poultry and meat, remember this one tip that will spare your palate: look for liquid in the bottom of the package. If there's liquid that means it was frozen and has now thawed. That liquid is the result of cells rupturing, releasing their liquid. Dreadful consequences for flavor!

Perfect Hard Boiled Eggs

How do you peel those hard-boiled eggs? It's Easy, Breezy! Crack the shell, *then* place in cool water. Cool water will enter the cracks, separating the egg white from the egg shell!

Waffles Perfected

How? In the tropics, here's a secret: when preparing waffle batter, mix in one tablespoon white wine into the batter. The cooking process will burn off the alcohol, but the wine will also prevent the batter from sticking to the hot surface. Guess who showed me that secret?

Tender Vegetables Every Time

On occasion you might have to add water to vegetables you are cooking. When that happens, make sure you add HOT water. Why? Because if you add cool or cold water, the abrupt temperature change will cause the vegetables to tighten—and toughen up.

Rest Meat Before Browning

Before you brown meat, let it acclimate to room temperature. Why? Meat at room temperature browns more evenly and retains more of its juices.

Onions before Garlic

If a recipe calls for sautéed garlic and onions, sauté the onions first, then the garlic. Otherwise, you run the risk of burning the garlic, which releases a bitter taste into the oil, making for sour-tasting onions!

Measurements for Making Jams

I am so old school sometimes! I still can fruit. Here is my handy list for arithmetic, which my mother handed down to me.

- *Apples*: 1 bushel (50 pounds) cans 17 to 20 quarts
- *Apricots*: 4 baskets or crates (1 bushel) cans 20 to 25 quarts

- *Berries*: 24 quart crate cans 15 to 24 quarts
- *Grapes*: 1 bushel (48 pounds) cans 16 to 20 quarts
- *Pears*: 1 bushel (58 pounds) cans 20 to 24 quarts
- *Peaches*: 1 bushel (50 pounds) cans 18 to 20 quarts
- *Pineapples*: 15 pineapples yields 30 pints
- *Plums*: 1 bushel (56 pounds) cans 24 to 30 quarts
- *Tomatoes*: 1 bushel (56 pounds) cans 15 to 20 quarts

Stocking a Pantry

A pantry with essentials is one sure way of saving money. Buy on sale, use when needed! How Easy, Breezy! Here is a list of items I find indispensable in the tropics.

- Assorted pasta shapes
- Baking chocolate squares
- Bottled water
- Canned tomatoes: whole, diced, crushed, pureed
- Capers
- Coffee, from Chiapas or Oaxaca
- Couscous
- Cornmeal
- Crackers, soda and other varieties
- Dijon mustard
- Dried and canned beans: cannellini, chickpeas, black, pinto
- Dried chiles
- Dried porcini mushrooms
- Extra virgin olive oil
- Flashlights, since power goes out so frequently
- Flour, white and whole wheat
- Imported, oil-packed tuna
- Kasha
- Lentils: brown and French green
- Marinated artichokes
- Olives
- Olive paste
- Quick-cooking polenta
- Red wine vinegar
- Rice: arborio and basmati
- Sugar, granular and confectioner's
- Sun-dried tomatoes
- Teas, caffeinated and herbal

- Tortilla, chips
- Vinegar: Balsamic, red, and white
- Wine, at least half a dozen bottles of wine

Freshen Guest Rooms

Guests arriving tomorrow on United's evening flight? Two days before they arrive, place a damp paper towel in a dish and add a couple of teaspoons of vanilla extract in the guest room. The vanilla will absorb that stale smell, and will make whichever flowers you then bring into the room smell that much more vibrant and tropical!

Princess is Parched!

And I am confident you could use a potent potable just about right now. I think I'll have a . . .

MARTINI

1 ¾ ounces London dry gin
½ ounce French (dry) vermouth (Noilly Prat)

Stir slowly but well in a mixing glass with generous amounts of ice. Strain into a chilled cocktail glass. Garnish with a chilled garlic onion, or with a thinly sliced onion. Olives? Perhaps, but never, ever for a martini you serve Hemingway!

Read *A Farewell to Arms* by Ernest Hemingway. Remember when Lieutenant Frederic Henry arrives in Stressa and takes a hotel room? "There was a big double bed, a *letto matrimoniale* with a satin coverlet. The hotel was very luxurious. I went down the long halls, down the wide stairs, through the rooms to the bar. I knew the barman and sat on a high stool and ate salted almonds and potato chips. The martini felt cool and clean." Then he starts up a conversation with Emilio, the barman, as he begins his second martini. But of course you knew that, didn't you?

Drink and read . . . responsibly!

WONDERFUL BEAUTY TIPS!

Did I tell you?

Isn't it always the case, we worry about things that never happen?

As you look at your life, how many times have you fretted over something or other? It began when you didn't do your homework and you thought it was the end of the world. Neither your teacher nor your parents killed you, did they?

Of course that's rhetorical! Had they killed you, you wouldn't be reading this!

I was reminded of this recently while going through a box with spiral notebooks. I stumbled upon an envelope filled with photographs. They were taken in December 1999 when we traveled to Miami for New Year's.

Remember the anticipation? The collective thrill? It was as if the entire world gasped not just for a new year and a new century, but a *New Millennium*! Oh, the promise of it all! Of course there was also the dread: Would computers work when December 31, 1999 became January 1, 2000?

Y2K had been hyped as a threat to the *World As We Knew It*!

Untold billions had been spent to make sure the world would go on. Or at least the world's computers! And without a hitch, all those years of worrying were for naught. The intrusive, disruptive, infuriating, and splendid computers all chugged along, fully capable of making the transition from "99" to "00" without skipping a nanosecond of nonsense.

My husband breathlessly awaited news reports that announced to the world that ATMs were working in Auckland . . . then Melbourne . . . then Singapore ... then Tokyo . . . and so forth, as the new year arrived around the world. Nonetheless, all afternoon we were waiting—fearing—that computers would, somewhere, fail. It didn't happen.

Hallelujah to all the geeks and nerds! My husband, for his part, toasted ATMs the world over. He raised a glass of champagne and pronounced, "My respects to Serendipity and Fortune! Here's to Virtue and Grace!"

It was a marvelous New Year's, witnessing as the world went from 1999 to 2000! Miami Beach, with its magnificent gaudiness and over-the-top vulgarity, was a thrill! How wonderful! I adored every moment of it all!

That this new century has proven to be a disappointment for humanity is another matter! You wouldn't think so by looking at the joyful faces in these pictures!

But enough about me and my photographs, let's move on to the matter at hand!

Wonderful Beauty Tips

Save Our Skin!

1. Oily skin? Here's a natural remedy that works wonders: mash a medium size banana and add one teaspoon honey and three drops of lemon juice. Mix and apply to your face. After 20 minutes, remove with a damp, cool washcloth.

2. Dry skin? One egg yolk, with a teaspoon each of honey and olive oil. Apply to your face and leave for 20 minutes. Then remove with a damp, cool washcloth.

3. Sunburned skin? Make green tea, add ice to cool it down. Soak a washcloth and cover your face. Sit back and rest for half hour. The green tea with soothe and heal sunburned skin naturally.

4. Sunburned skin? Mix plain yogurt with oatmeal. Apply to your skin. Sit back and rest for half hour. The yogurt with soothe and heal sunburned skin naturally.

5. Soothe stressed out skin with this simple remedy: mash half a ripe avocado with a teaspoon aloe vera. Slice a medium sized cucumber. Apply the avocado mash to your face and place cucumber slices over your eyes. Relax for about half hour. When the avocado is dry to the touch, remove with a damp, cool washcloth.

Hand Care

1. If you garden, put cotton balls in each finger of your gloves. This will protect your nails and cuticles, saving a bundle over the years in manicures.

2. A simple recipe to relax your tired hands after a long day in the tropics is simple: one cup warm water, one cup aloe vera, the juice and pulp of one cucumber. (In a blender pour both cups and add one cucumber—without the seeds—and blend.) Soak your hands. The aloe vera and cucumber will do wonders!

Healthier Teeth

A set of healthier teeth can be yours by eating more mushrooms. Although nothing substitutes for good oral hygiene, mushrooms contain compounds that fight bacteria growth in the mouth.

Clean Breath

One cup water, ½ teaspoon salt, and ½ teaspoon baking soda is all you need to make a mouth wash. Gargle, rinse, and you won't need Scope or Listerine.

Ease Away Vertigo

How? Use your index and middle fingers to press down on the groove between the tendons that run from the base of your palm to your wrist. I was told about this Easy, Breezy tip when I became dizzy after climbing one of the pyramids of Mayapán! That's how the Maya keep their balance while dancing atop their gorgeous temples and pyramids!

Eat Mint

And not just the mint in your mojito! Grow it in your garden! Add it to your soups! Mix it in your salad greens! The more, the better! Mint has been shown to improve the flow of bile and to reduce acid reflux. Now you know!

Cranberry and Prune Juice

Yes, I admit it! There is one thing that I insist on doing myself: making cranberry juice or tea! I then combine with prune juice. These wonderful fruit prevent urinary tract infections, which become a greater concern as we age.

Wart Away!

An unusual remedy for warts is peculiar but effective: duct tape! Yes! Tape the wart every day for a week or so. No one knows how it works. It is speculated that the adhesive in the duct tape irritates the skin and triggers an immune reaction that fights the infection associated with most warts.

Healthier Feet

After an especially hot day—did someone say the thermometer zipped past 100 Fahrenheit again?—protect your feet by soaking them for 15 minutes in a solution of cool water, salt, and rubbing alcohol. This combination will revitalize your feet—and kill odor-causing bacteria.

Avocado

Did you know that avocados are also known as the fertility fruit? Did you know they are indigenous to Mexico? Did you know they are rich in monounsaturated fats and vitamin E? Did you know that eating avocado once a day is a sure way of promoting supple, healthy skin?

Blister or Boil?

Soak the affected area in the bathtub—but add one cup oatmeal. The oatmeal will draw out the infection and leave the area far smoother.

Take the Sting Out of Insect Bites

Be it a wasp or a bee, running a bit of lemon juice on an insect bite neutralizes the venom—and makes you feel better!

Hairspray to the Rescue

1. After you have your shoes shined, just spray them with a little hairspray. They will keep their shine and repel dust!
2. What works for your shoes, also works for stockings! Spray them lightly and you'll reduce significantly the chance that they will run.

Whiten Nails

If you soak your fingers in warm water and lemon juice, the lemon juice will strip away stains. After 15 minutes, wash hands. You can protect your nails further by applying clear polish!

A Sauna for Face and Neck

Bring a pot of water to simmer, just so steam is rising. Add a few drops of essential oils—Coqui Coqui has divine scents—and place a towel over your head. Place your face at a comfortable position from the pot—usually around 12 inches or 30 centimeters and inhale slowly for a couple of minutes. The steam will soothe your skin. Here are recommended essential oils to go with specific skin types. NORMAL skin: mandarin and lavender; OILY skin: lemon and eucalyptus; and for DRY skin: rose and chamomile.

Moisturize Skin with Avocado Oil

Blessed Mexico, which gave us avocados! Apart from guacamole, did you know that avocado oil has more nutrients for your skin than the most expensive moisturizers? Massage a drop of avocado oil into your hands, wrists, elbows, and knees and you will be on your way to reducing the effects of aging and reversing sun damage!

Age Spots—Banished!

What we call age spots are often simply dead skin cells. A little lemon juice rubbed into your skin will dry them out. Then use a gentle body scrub and wash your hands as usual. Over time, the age spots will almost disappear completely.

Extend the Life of Perfumes

In the tropics, it is certainly warmer! And nothing affects the volatile oils in fine perfume than this heat. Rather than displaying your treasured perfumes on your dresser, here's an Easy, Breezy tip: store them in your refrigerator! The integrity of the scent will last far, far longer!

Lemon Your Bath

Rather than spending a fortune on bath salts, you can make your own with this great recipe: draw your bath and pour half a cup of regular salt. Then add the juice of two lemons! The salt and lemon will work wonders toning your skin while you bathe!

Lighten Your Hair

If you're blonde or have light brown hair, you can get terrific highlights with lemon juice. After you shampoo, you can use a wedge to run through strands you want lightened, then sit in the sun. No harsh chemicals and it can be a fun thing to do with a friend!

Natural Headache Reliever

Did you know that slices of cucumber and lemon in a glass of water work to alleviate pain? Slight headaches and muscle aches will vanish with a glass of water thus treated!

Diminish Varicose Veins

Whenever I want to primp for my Bettie Page imitation, a few days beforehand I work on diminishing varicose veins! How do I do it? Simple: a few drops of lemon and avocado oil, equal parts, are massage into the varicose veins . . . and if they don't disappear they certainly do diminish!

Reduce Dandruff!

Here's a secret formula: mix two tablespoons lime juice in two cups water. Rinse into your hair, letting it dry. You will reduce dandruff flakes!

Skin Toning

1. With lemon juice? Of course! Simply dab a few lemon drops on your face. Remove with cotton balls. The lemon juice will kill bacteria and tone your complexion as do most astringents.

2. Isn't papaya wonderful? Of course it is! It is also a wonderful skin toner. How? Rub some papaya onto your skin. Let dry. Then gently rinse your face with warm water and a washcloth.

Gentle Exfoliate

1. Mix oatmeal with water and a few drops of your favorite essential oil—lavender and eucalyptus—until you have a gritty paste. Apply in a circular motion. There you are, an exfoliate money can't buy.

2. Olive oil and sea salt. Mix until you are content with the grittiness. Apply in a circular motion. There you are, an exfoliate money can't buy.

Reducing Calluses Between Pedicures

1. Don't think me mad when I make this suggestion on removing calluses, because it works! Before you go to bed, massage chest vapor rub—yes, chest vapor rub!—into your calluses. Then put on socks to prevent staining your bed sheets. Do this several nights in a row and the calluses will vanish over the course of a week or so.

2. This is a simple way of keeping calluses from forming. Mix one gallon of water into a container appropriate for soaking your feet. Add one cup lemon juice, ½ cup milk, and ¼ cup olive oil. Mix thoroughly and soak your feet for 20 minutes.

Easy, Breezy Nail Care

The wonderful thing about Mexico is that there are several varieties of mayonnaise for sale—including ones with lemon juice! If you get in the habit of once a week scooping a little of the lemon-enriched mayonnaise in a cup and using it to "moisturize" your fingernails and cuticles, you will be surprised how soft your cuticles become—and how shiny your nails will shimmer.

Spiffy Up Your Fingernails

If you rub a wedge of lime or lemon on your fingernails you will accomplish two things. First, you will soften your cuticles, making it easier to trim your nails. Second, you will whiten the enamel, making for more brilliant nails!

Bergdorf Goodman Be Gone!

It happens to the best of us every now and then! Yes, we dab too much perfume and we smell like the main floor at Bergdorf Goodman! Ghastly! Here's a secret that Audrey Hepburn once showed me: dab the spot with a cotton ball that's been moistened with rubbing alcohol. It works!

Running Low on Your Favorite Perfume?

In the reverse case, and you have just about run out of your favorite scent, try this: apply a thin layer of petroleum jelly on your skin, THEN dab on the perfume. The petroleum jelly will distribute the scent's oils evenly on your skin—and make the fragrance last longer!

Fennel Reduces Gas

Fennel is a splendid vegetable and fennel seeds are wonderful spices. Stock up and use often and there's an added bonus: fennel seeds are a carminative, which relieve gas! How's that for a natural way to aid digestion!

Chaya in Your Soup

Whatever non-cream soup you are making, add chaya at the end as if it were spinach. This is an excellent source of iron, calcium, and vitamin C. Abundant and inexpensive, it packs a punch when it comes to antioxidants associated with healthier skin and improved eyesight.

Alleviate Nighttime Coughing

Here in the tropics, gorgeous honey abounds! Here's a bonus: save hundreds of dollars over the years by remembering that honey is more effective at quelling nighttime coughing than most over-the-counter cough syrups! Now you know.

Strengthen Bones

As time goes by, so does the calcium in our bones—which leaches out! Make sure you eat lots of low-fat dairy products, cruciferous vegetables, and beans.

Cleaning Tweezers, Nail Clippers, and Metallic Beauty Aids

The recipe: place items in a bowl. Fill with water. Drop in a denture-cleaning effervescent tablet!

Soothe a Sore Throat

A time-tested solution for a sore throat: ¼ cup lemon juice and ¼ cup water. Mix and gargle. You will fight bacteria while soothing your irritated throat!

Instant Hand Sanitizer

Why waste money on hand sanitizers? Here's a recipe: two cups aloe vera gel, two teaspoons rubbing alcohol, and one teaspoon of your favorite oil (lavender or eucalyptus are perennial favorites). Mix well and put in a hand soap dispenser. There you are, ready to sanitize your hands in an Easy, Breezy way.

Hair and Skin Moisturizer

A favorite recipe: one mashed banana, two tablespoons sour cream, and one tablespoon honey. Mix ingredients and apply to your face. Air dry for 20 minutes. Rinse clean!

Brighten That Smile

Back to the kitchen! One teaspoon baking soda, one teaspoon salt, and one teaspoon dried sage are all you need to make a natural teeth whitener. Dip a moistened toothbrush and brush as usual.

Instant, Subtle Lip Treatment

Squeeze a few drops of your favorite berry or fruit and mix with a bit of petroleum jelly. Dab on your lips for an instant and subtle lip gloss!

Body Scrub

Here's a terrific scrub for your neck, back, ankles, and feet: one tablespoon coffee grounds and one tablespoon salt. Mix in a bowl and use as a scrub in the shower. Rinse and moisturize when done.

Gentle Exfoliate

Regular sugar and a few drops of water are all you need to make a gentle exfoliate that's ideal for your forehead, nose, and cheeks. Once a week!

Moisturize Your Hair

Did you know that if you warm up olive oil, massage it into your hair, wrap a towel around it for half an hour, and then wash your hair you will end up with properly moisturized, soft hair? Now you do!

Sleek Hair

How? In the tropics, it's Easy, Breezy with this recipe: ¼ cup milk and two tablespoons honey. Mix and apply to your hair for half hour, then shampoo with a gentle shampoo.

Reduce Dandruff

1. How? Beat the whites of two eggs (no yolks!) and a cup of yogurt. Mix and apply to hair and scalp. Sit back for half hour, then wash out with warm water.

2. How? Mix a quarter cup vinegar and a few drops ginger juice. Apply to scalp for 15 minutes, then shampoo.

Protect Your Wrists!

How? In the tropics, I've found that rubbing almond oil into my wrists reduces age spots and minimizes wrinkles.

Lemons and Sweets

Tempted by sweets? Did you know that a whiff of lemon—inhale the scent of the rind—will immediately diminish your craving for sweets? It works!

Healthy Water

A slice of lemon or lime in your drinking water will help your body remove toxins. Get in the habit of drinking lime- or lemon-scented water. You will be invigorated and enjoy improved health.

Heal Canker Sores

If you mix the juice of one lemon and lukewarm water, then rinse your mouth three times a day, you will accelerate the healing time for canker sores. Now you know.

Adding Lemon to Teas . . .

. . . Is one Easy, Breezy remedy for reducing chills and fevers. Drink lemon-enriched tea every two hours.

An Instant Energy Booster

If you bite into a lemon, the rush of this citrus will give you a natural energy boost—who needs to squander money on energy bars when this is such a simple remedy! Of course you know to drink water afterward, to remove acid from your teeth's enamel.

Protect Your Vital Organs!

Drop a few slices of radishes in your water and a few mint leaves. The radishes and mint will provide wonderful nutrients to your organs as you drink water throughout the day!

Brighter Eyes

How? In the tropics, remember that all this sun makes us all squint! It's imperative to give your eye muscles a rest . . . and nothing is more relaxing that slices of cool cucumber over your closed eyes for at least 20 minutes each day.

Drink Tea

If you drink tea once a day, you will aid digestion and restore your skin's natural balance which is undermined by tropical heat. Oolong tea and sorrel teas, for instance, contain polyphenols that are wonderful.

Peppermint Oil

Why squander money on pain killers when most headaches can be eliminated by hydrating—a glass of herbal tea—and rubbing peppermint oil into your temples. Proper hydration and the menthol soothe headaches in no time.

Eat Ginger

A natural decongestion is easily made by pouring two cups boiling water over a teaspoon of grated ginger. Strain. Then add a pinch of cayenne pepper. Sip slowly.

Bitters

Did I mention that olives, endive, and radicchio are natural remedies for sugar cravings? Eat more of these, and your body will want fewer sweets! In these tropical climates, that means fewer cavities, fewer calories, and fewer health problems!

Support Your Feet

They support you, don't they? Get in the habit of buying a pair of brand new sneakers with good arch support every three months. Merle Greene Robertson insisted that was her secret. She lived to be almost 98—and was still climbing pyramids!

Lower Blood Pressure

That's easy as *uno, dos, tres*. How? Simple! Make potassium-rich foods part of your life! Bananas, oranges, and cantaloupe should be part of your breakfast every single day! That's Easy, Breezy!

Facial Massage

As important as a facial mask is a facial massage! Of course you knew that, but everyone needs a reminder once in a while. Here's your reminder! The next time you get a massage, and you should at least twice a month, ask your therapist if he or she is trained in myofascial release or neuromuscular therapy. If she or he isn't, get a recommendation! There are the trigger points in the face, cranium, and neck that need to be indulged.

Rosemary Bushes

How many of my tips include rosemary? The scent of rosemary is linked with improved memory! Plant rosemary bushes and you will have a wonderful herb that will make it unnecessary to spend money on computer games to sharpen your mind!

Good Bacteria, Bad Bacteria

Bacteria adore the tropics! They do, don't they? Not all bacteria are good, however. Make sure that the good varieties (*Lactobacillus* or *Bifidobacterium*) thrive in your digestive system. How? Eat yogurt with active cultures, kimchi (sold at various gourmet and natural foods shops around town), and indulge in laban with cucumber (Byblos Restaurant at the Lebanese Social Club offers the best!).

Lavender

If you are going to have rosemary bushes in your home, then you might as well have lavender. Why? Lavender flowers in your bath and your bedroom are a natural way to relax—and enjoy sound sleep. Wake up rejuvenated, ready to enjoy the day!

A Natural Immunity Boost

Here is a natural remedy that continues to amaze: garlic. Indeed! The antiviral and antibacterial properties of garlic are best harvested by habitually eating raw or lightly cooked garlic at least for one meal a day.

Tailored Clothes

Buying "off the rack" is perfectly fine, but in many tropical countries, there are wonderful tailors. Here in Mérida, there's no reason why you can't have your clothes fitted to your individual measurements. You will look so much better—and for men, there's no reason why you shouldn't have a few *guayaberas* custom made. You will look that much more dashing than if you simply walk around in a Golden Fleece shirt from Brooks Brothers!

Hot Oil Hair Treatment for Men

Once a month, warm up ¼ olive oil with a rosemary twig. Work into your man's hair, and let sit for 15 minutes. Then shampoo regularly. This hot oil treatment will do wonders for his hair and scalp—and keep follicles stronger longer!

Manicures/Pedicures for Men

Believe it or not, regular manicures and pedicures are a terrific investment, since they will prevent rough, callused hands and feet—and the problems they cause down the road.

Facial Masks for Men

1. The simplest facial treatment for men is to combine baking soda and water to make a thin paste. Apply to face and let dry. Rinse in warm water. This will exfoliate skin and tighten pores.

2. If you have sun damage on your face—and in the tropics just about every man does—use this recipe. Mix two egg yolks and apply to your face, let dry. Egg yolks have Vitamin A which alleviates sun damage in an Easy, Breezy way!

3. Combine oatmeal and honey for a natural facial scrub. Slowly rub into your face in a circular motion. Let dry for about 20 minutes. Rinse your face in cool water.

Body Scrub for Men

Mix sea salt, a few drops of essential oil—eucalyptus or rosemary are both wonderful—and a few drops of water. This will reinvigorate your neck, shoulders, chest, and torso. Great for calves and feet as well.

Princess is Parched!

And I am confident you could use a potent potable just about right now. I think I'll have a . . .

SANGRIA

1 liter dry red wine
Juice of 2 limes or lemons
Juice of two oranges
¼ inch slices of lemons and oranges, to taste

Stir slowly all ingredients in a pitcher. Let sit in the sun for a hour or two. Fill highball glasses with ice, pour and garnish with fruit.

Read *The Dangerous Summer* by Ernest Hemingway. Who can forget that, after the bullfighting spectacle is over, Hemingway and his entourage head out to Pepica's where they enjoy "sangria, red wine with fresh oranges and lemon juice in it, served in big pitchers." What a splendid way to spend an afternoon in the tropics! But of course you knew that, didn't you?

Drink and read . . . responsibly!

WONDERFUL PET CARE TIPS!

Did I tell you?

When I first started this conversation with you, writing a book, I mentioned that when we left Cuba, we never looked back.

I suppose this is technically correct, but there's more to it than that.

We did miss Cuba and it would be wrong to deny it. We cultivated Cuban friends in Mexico. We hosted Americans we had befriended in Havana. We followed, with dismay, the news as that island-nation descended into madness.

Who would have thought that our old haunts would be razed to build a horrid housing project for those Soviet and East European Communists, right in the heart of Vedado? Madness, all of it!

But I will tell you this, we delighted in hosting Cuban friends like Leopoldo Fernández, who was the radio and television star "Tres Patines." He carried on with his show in Veracruz before he settled in Miami. If you're not sure who he is, look him up on YouTube: "Tres Patines" or "La Tremenda Corte."

We'd sail to Veracruz for song and nostalgia—my husband adored María Antonia Peregrino Álvarez. She was more commonly known as Toña la Negra. What a voice! Her interpretations of boleros and rumbas are without equal. Although she became a national sensation with her interpretation of "Enamorada," our favorite was "Cenizas." YouTube her if you must!

Darling, in Veracruz we would visit Leopoldo Fernández. Once, he sailed back with us from Veracruz for a long weekend—whatever that is, I'm not sure. In any case, when we arrived here, oh, the fun! It was all there: the company, the laughter, the exquisite seafood, and the drinks. By that time, mind you, the pool had been finished and the entire place had been properly appointed.

My husband had invited other Cubans for that weekend—the men were busy with a *lechón asado a la criolla*, *congri* and *yuca*—for the midday feast and, of course, mojitos. But it was still early one morning when Leopoldo found his way to the veranda off his bedroom. He was smoking a cigar, a Cohiba. He had never had *huevos motuleños* before. He adored them.

I approached and startled him. (That we, now in Yucatán, had three Airedale Terrier dogs, as we had in Havana, was comforting to our Cuban guests who commented on the continuity of our lifestyle from one tropical paradise to another tropical paradise.) Then he turned around and, for a moment, I saw it!

Yes, after I startled him, he turned around, and there was *that look* on his face!

"It happens to me, too," I said quietly.

"What happens?" he asked.

"There are times when I quickly glance up and, for a moment, my mind plays tricks on me."

"Oh," he said.

"Yes, the way the pool is set back from the terrace, the shape of the arches leading off the veranda, the way the bougainvillea drapes over the wrought iron. In the right light, at the right moment, I glance quickly—and it's as if I'm transported back to Vedado."

He smiled. He looked off in the distance.

"*Eso fue otra vida*," he said. "That was another life. We'll never live that way again."

He paused. A moment later he added, "There's something to be said for a world that allows you live different lives during the same lifetime. *Cosa más grande en la vida . . .*"

"Cenizas" played softly in the background, amid the laughter of men tending the grill. Our Airedale Terriers dashed about, chasing each other, oblivious to the melancholy of what's been gained and what's been lost. It would turn out to be a set of glorious days, with good food, good friends, and good times. That's how things should be, here in this glorious land of the Mayab.

But enough about me and my nostalgic Cuban houseguests, let's move on to the matter at hand!

Wonderful Pet Care Tips

Bath Time Secret

Most dogs hate baths because bathtubs are slippery. Solution? Place a towel on the bottom of the tub and then slowly fill with water. The towel will provide the necessary traction to keep your dog calm while you bathe him—saving you the cost of a professional groomer!

Bathing a Cat?

Yikes! Good luck with that! Instead, try this: gently work cornstarch into your cat's fur. Cornstarch will absorb body oils, perspiration, odors, and dirt. And with a few simple brushes—not to mention your cat's natural tendency to lick constantly—you'll achieve the same result.

Keep Fleas Off your Pets

A natural alternative to flea and tick collars is simple: sprinkle a few drops of natural lavender oil in your pet's sleeping area. Fleas will flee—and your pet will thank you.

Pet Hair Solutions

1. A fresh fabric softener sheet can be used to wipe cat and dog hair off furniture and fabrics. Simply wipe the furniture, cushions, and area rugs. The fabric softener sheet will also help prevent more shed hair from sticking to these surfaces.

2. If your favorite sofa or seat is covered in cat or dog hair, simply put on a pair of dishwashing gloves. Run your hands over the sofa seat or cushions and through the magic of static electricity, the hair will cling to the rubber dishwashing gloves.

3. After you brush your cat or dog, run a dryer sheet over their fur. The static cling will pick up stray hairs—and keep fur in place!

Extend the Life of Cat Litter

Don't throw away those used tea bags! Dry them out, then cut them open and recycle the tea in your cat litter. The dried tea leaves will extend the life of your cat litter.

Neat and Tidy Litter Boxes

If you put the litter box on top of a sisal area rug, you will greatly reduce the mess that happens when cats enter and leave the boxes. Added bonus? The sisal rug will file down your cat's claws on a continuing basis!

Cheap Flea Prevention

After consulting your veterinarian, try this: use Lever 2000 deodorant soap to wash your dog! It worked like magic for us!

Killing Fleas

Did you know that crushed moth balls sprinkled on pillows, carpets, and blankets that are infested with fleas will kill off those parasites? Now you do! Then vacuum to make sure you rid your home of any dormant eggs that may linger.

Save on Litter

Line your litter box with a plastic bag. Then place the litter. This will make for easy clean up and prevent urine from seeking to the bottom of the container, creating unpleasant odors.

Keep Dogs From Licking

In the heat, dogs have a tendency to lick themselves to the point of irritating their skin! Poor creatures! But if you dab a bit of Crisco, they will refrain from licking that part of their skin. That will save you the cost of a trip to the veterinarian. Now you know!

Tangled Fur?

If you sprinkle talcum powder, it's far easier to brush your pet's fur. That, of course, and patience!

Grooming Savings

How? Make a deal! Did you know the slowest days for most groomers are Tuesdays and Wednesdays? Make a deal with your groomer: get a discount if you take your dog to be groomed on a Tuesday or Wednesday. That's what we've done—at a saving of about 40 percent off the regular price.

Litter for Less?

Not quite, but you will use less litter if get in the habit of mixing in some baby powder—the litter will remain odor free longer, meaning you will use less of it over time!

Cedar in the Litter

Here in the tropics, cedar chips are a saving grace! Sprinkle some in the cat's litter box and you will do everyone in your household a favor!

End the Clawing!

Whatever your cat is scratching can be saved by mixing a tablespoon of hot sauce—as if that were difficult to find in the tropics—and a cup of water. Just spray on the surface of whatever Miss Kitty is scratching. Why does it work? Darling, cats hate hot sauce!

Freshen Up Pooch's Bed

A dry fabric softener will reduce the smell of dogs, especially around his or her bed and favorite blanket. Works wonderfully!

Cajole Your Cat to Sleep Where You Want

If your cat insists on jumping onto the sofa and curling up on your favorite pillow, here's a solution that's time tested. Simply throw a towel into the dryer and then fold and place where you want the cat to sleep. The warm towel will be a nice and cozy retreat.

Lemons Banish Fleas

One cup water, one cup lemon juice and a spray bottle are all you need for a natural solution to spray on your dog—mindful to stay clear of your pet's face—to rid your pooch of fleas!

Keep Cats Away . . . Naturally

If your cat insists on biting the leaves of your favorite houseplants, the remedy is easy. Rub the leaves with a wedge of lemon, and when it dries, cats will stay clear—they hate the taste of lemons.

Keep Dogs Away... Naturally

If your dog insists on meddling in your favorite flower pots, just sprinkle some cayenne pepper—the smell repels dogs and won't harm your flowering plants.

Perfect Paws

Using moist baby wipes is a simple way to clean your pet's paws—before they jump onto the sofa.

Healthier Skin and Coat = Less Dander

Check with your veterinarian first, of course, and if you are given the green light, an Easy, Breezy way of reducing dander, while giving your pet healthier skin and shinier coat, is to mix in one raw egg in their food once a week—or sprinkle the oil found in one can of sardines. The omega-3 fatty oils are often all that's missing in your pet's diet. But always check with your veterinarian first!

Calming Nervous Pets

Believe it or not, you are a calming influence on your pet! Whenever they are stressed, such as when they are being taken to the veterinarian or groomer—or on a plane ride—make sure you take along a piece of laundry with your scent. A T-shirt is perfect, since your pet will find your scent in a pet carrier or at the groomer's place a calming presence.

United Flight 1427... or Any Flight!

Rather than filling the water dish or dispenser with water, fill it with ice! It won't splash, and it will last longer, since your pet will be able to lick the ice cube throughout the course of the flight from here to there.

Calmer Pets... As You Drive About!

Calm your pet by using the all-natural, time-tested Bach's Rescue Remedy. Just add a few drops to your cat's or dog's water bowl—or on a treat—and their nerves will calm down. Use as necessary, since it's all natural. I know of three shops in Mérida that carry it—Google it!

Cleaner Teeth and Healthier Gums—Free!

Any of the local markets around town that have butchers will be happy to give you a few pork bones. Thoroughly cook these in any kind of stock—chicken or beef—and your dog will be in heaven. As your dog chews the bones, plaque will be removed from teeth and gums will be strengthened. This is an Easy, Breezy solution to better canine oral care—for free!

Fresher Breath

If you're not thrilled by the idea of giving your dog a bone to remove plaque build-up naturally, you can simply add chopped fresh parsley to his or her food. Parsley cleans breath—of dogs, cats, and also people!

Cleaning the Cat Litter Box

When it's time to replace litter, make sure your rinse the box with one cup warm water and one cup white vinegar. Let stand for an hour. Rinse, dry, and fill with fresh litter. The litter box will stay fresher for a longer period of time.

Fresher-Smelling Litter Boxes

And of course, you can always sprinkle talcum powder into cat litter to extend the life of the litter by keeping it smelling fresher for a longer period of time.

Wait, Wait . . . Don't Tell Me!

Yes, it's true! NPR (National Public Radio) is the most soothing radio station . . . so simply tune your Internet radio to those liberal voices from Washington, D.C. when you leave your home and your dog or cat will be calmed by the monotone delivery of those taxpayer-subsidized voices.

Keep the Dog from Chewing?

How? It's Easy, Breezy if you spray whatever is being chewed—after you ensure it is colorfast—with a combination of water and lemon juice. Dogs loathe citrus!

Dogs' Ear Infections

Always check first with your veterinarian . . . but after spending a small fortune every time one of our dogs developed ear infections, a friend suggested something that has worked wonders: over the counter cream for vaginal yeast infection! It's true!

"Bathing" Your Cat

Does your cat hate being washed? Of course your cat hates being washed! But in the tropics, it's vital that your pet stay clean. Here's the secret, darling: gently rub your cat with baby wipes—and then brush the cat's fur!

Cleaning up Accident Sites

How? In the tropics, cleanliness is next to being spectacular! How do I achieve this? Well, whenever a pet has an accident—and they will since they are only human, so to speak—just pour white vinegar on the spot! It cleans, it disinfects, and it's cheap!

Cheap Dog Toys...

It takes two steps. Step 1: Go to any store that sells cheap toys for piñatas. Step 2: Recycle old socks that have lost their pair, or have holes. Then stuff a piñata stuffer or two. Tie a knot. Your dog will have a new toy, all for a few pesos!

Keep Ants Away...

From your pet's food bowl. How, you ask? Rub a little petroleum jelly around the base of the bowl, and then sprinkle cinnamon. Ants detest cinnamon and will not crawl up the side of your pet's food bowl.

Princess is Parched!

And I am confident you could use a potent potable just about right now. I think I'll have a . . .

NEGRONI

1 ounce dry gin
1 ounce Campari
1 ounce Italian (sweet) vermouth
Orange twist for garnish

Stir the ingredients, except the orange twist, in a mixing glass. Strain into a chilled cocktail glass. Garnish.

Read *Across the River and Into the Trees* by Ernest Hemingway. I'm confident you remember how, in "The Good Lion," Hemingway writes, "But the good lion would sit and fold his wings and ask politely if he might have a Negroni or an Americano." A Negroni is something you should also demand at least once a month! But of course you knew that, didn't you?

Drink and read . . . responsibly!

WONDERFUL EVERYDAY HOUSEHOLD & CAR TIPS!

Did I tell you?

I was in New York recently. My sister lives in Newport, Rhode Island and we always get together at least twice a year. It was my turn to travel to her. It was a delightful visit, but it put me in a nostalgic mood.

Why?

One of the things we did was take in a few Broadway shows—Alec Baldwin was terrific in *Orphans*. I am still thinking about the arresting Fiona Shaw in *The Testament of Mary*. What I can say with a most definite certainty is that this is the first time I have seen birds of prey on a Broadway stage. I'm disappointed that New Yorkers allowed this play to flop on Broadway. Who wouldn't want to see a play in which the Virgin Mary rejects the divinity of her son? I thought there would be enough New Yorkers curious enough to keep the play going for its scheduled run. I was mistaken!

But there's no doubt that *Pippin*, however cheesy, is a sentimental favorite. It was wonderful to see Andrea Martin play Berthe, the grandmother. The first time I saw *Pippin* was in 1973—exactly four decades ago! Oh, how the decades slip through your fingers. They do have a way of doing that, don't they?

Back in 1973, it was who played Berthe. Irene Ryan, although an accomplished stage actress, is best remembered for portraying Granny in *The Beverly Hillbillies* on television. Ben Vereen became a star as the Leading Player in that production.

One thing I will say is that today's young actors and actresses are certainly fit. I had forgotten the stamina required for musicals. Even in the revival of "Hair" I was surprised to see how much leaping and gymnastics were involved. In the current production of "Pippin," I do have a confession to make! I gasped at the gorgeous Orion Griffiths! Oh, my goodness . . . as the song says: "Give me a man who is handsome and strong!"

Darling, *I've have more than a month to get ready*! Google Orion Griffiths and you'll see what I mean.

My sister and I both laughed at my silliness, the way I went on about Mr.

Griffiths. Imagine the sight of a ridiculous old woman working her fingers all over her tablet, Googling him, looking up pictures of the gorgeous Mr. Griffiths on the Internet, over after-theater drinks at the Surrey Hotel, where we were staying, on East 76th Street.

We were like a couple of teenage girls giggling over a gorgeous boy! Good for us!

As the song says: "Makes me feel young all over!"

Stay young!

But enough about me and my wishful lusting, let's move on to the matter at hand!

Wonderful Everyday Household & Car Tips

On television sets and computer screens . . .

Simply wipe a fabric softener sheet across the flat screen, whether it's your television, computer, laptop or Kindle. The fabric softeners will eliminate almost all the static electricity that draws dust to the glass.

Dust on Blinds

There are two ways to minimize dust on your Persian blinds. One is to rub a fresh fabric softener the length of the blinds. The other is to spray static guard on the blinds.

Mildew on Books

In the tropics, however careful one may be, books do get mildew. The solution? Gently sprinkle unscented talcum powder or corn starch on the mildewed pages, and close the book. The powder or starch will absorb the moisture and dry out the mildew. A few days later, simply brush off the powder or corn starch.

Cat Litter in your Library?

Need to keep your library smelling fresh in the tropics? Who doesn't? Here's a simple time-tested solution. Sprinkle cat litter—yes! Sprinkle cat litter all over the floor. Close up the room. Wait 48 hours, and then vacuum. The cat litter will have absorbed the musty scent—and reduces the number of spores responsible for mildew and mold.

Cleaner Pools . . . with Tennis Balls!

What? Yes, it's true. Toss a tennis ball . . . and it will absorb all the oil—suntan lotion and body oils—floating on the surface of the water. It will keep your pool cleaner, longer. And of course, you can simply toss the tennis ball in your washing machine!

Keep Ants Out of the Kitchen

How do you get rid of those pesky ants? Easy! Pour a little cinnamon in a spray bottle, add water, shake, and spray your kitchen counters and window sills. The ants detest cinnamon and will stay away. A completely wonderful, easy, green solution!

Keep Mice Away

If you sprinkle baking soda around the corners where mice hide, they will stay away. They hate baking soda!

Keep Bugs Out of your Bathroom

Who needs insect repellants when this solution works as well: one part rubbing alcohol and three parts water, and a spray bottle is all you need. Shake and spray anywhere in your bathroom. Bugs will be repelled.

Keep Bugs Away from Your Terrace Furniture

A simple solution to keep bugs from your terrace is this remedy: six drops vanilla extract and one cup water. Combine them in a spray bottle. Spray all your furniture. The bugs will stay clear of your terrace furniture.

Keep Bugs Away from Your Potted Flowers

If your beautiful flowers attract unwanted insects, here's a solution. Mix two tablespoons garlic powder with two cups water. Pour in a spray bottle, shake. Spray your flowers. The subtle scent of garlic will keep most bugs away from your flowers.

Keep Produce Clean and Crisp

For leafy greens, soak in water and add a teaspoon baking soda. Rinse and your salad will be perfectly clean.

Keeping Wood Floor Shining

The tropical sun can be unforgiving on wood floors. A simple solution is to mix equal parts vegetable oil (Mazola) and white vinegar in a spray bottle. Shake and spray. Then wipe with a clean cloth. Your wood floors will gleam.

Hiding Scratches on Wood Furniture

To hide scratches, there are two simple solutions. First, brew a strong pot of coffee and use a cotton ball to apply the strong coffee to the scratch. Second, use shoe polish. Whichever solution you opt for, simply blend in the coffee or shoe polish with a cotton ball.

Water Stains on Wood

Make a paste using two tablespoons vegetable oil and three tablespoons baking soda. Use this paste to rub gently over the water stain. Let it sit for about an hour or two. Then gently wipe away. If your stained furniture is very delicate, you may want to use mayonnaise instead. Simply use a paper towel to spread a light layer of mayonnaise over the water stain. Leave it for 12 hours. Then wipe clean with a damp cloth.

Easy Microwave Cleaning

Moisten a couple of paper towels and add one teaspoon lemon juice. Place in microwave and run on HIGH for three to four minutes. The steam and lemon juice will soften all the grime, making for an easy cleanup.

Cast-Iron Pan

Sea salt and a soft washcloth are all that you need to clean a cast-iron pan. When done, coat the inside with cooking oil. It's that Easy, Breezy!

Cleaner Coffeemaker Pots

How does Cenote Sally keep her glass coffeemaker pot crystal clear? This is the secret: fill the coffeemaker pot half with ice, mix the juice of one lemon, and add two tablespoons salt. Swirl for a couple of minutes. The ice, lemon juice, and salt will remove that unsightly blotchy haze!

Cleaning Coffee Grinders

The most effective way of cleaning coffee grinders is to grind up uncooked white rice. This removes all buildup, and the rice absorbs scents—fantastic if you use your coffee grinder to grind spcies!

Oven Stains

For stubborn oven stains, set your oven to WARM. Then turn off and cover stain with ketchup. It speaks of the acidity of ketchup when you notice how quickly it loosens and dissolves that stubborn stain! Wipe clean and dry.

Freshen Garbage Disposal, Part I

If your garbage disposal begins to smell—and it might as summer heats up—run a cup of ice and half a cup of white vinegar. That almost always does the trick.

Freshen Garbage Disposal, Part I

Another approach? Pour in a can of room temperature soda. The phosphoric acid strips away the odor-causing buildup in your disposal.

Orange Peel Membranes

Did you know that the membranes in oranges are perfect for polishing stainless steel? The natural oils will work wonders on kitchen sinks and faucets!

Cleaning Marble

The simplest solution for making marble shine like new? White chalk!

Pulverize a piece of chalk. Yes, the kind children use on blackboards! When this chalk dust is sprinkled on the marble, you will be able to rub it into the marble, then wipe clean with a damp cloth.

Cleaning Computer Keyboards

Oh, that's Easy, Breezy! Dip a Q-tip in hydrogen peroxide and run between the keys—while you're not online! The last thing you want to do is send off that angry email by mistake!

Cleaning your Desk

The most effective way of cleaning—and disinfecting—your desk . . . *I don't want to know what's stained your desk after so many tawdry hours on Facebook and Live Cam . . . but wiping it down with rubbing alcohol is the way to go.*

Tarnished Brass

Heavily tarnished brass can be cleaned in an Easy, Breezy way using this formula: 1/3 cup white vinegar and 1/4 cup flour. Mix and use this solution to polish any brass item. The vinegar will clean the tarnish and the flour will provide a gentle abrasive. If the item has heavy ornamentation, you may want to use a Q-tip.

Carpet Stains

For most organic stains—such as those from a pet's accident—if your carpet is colorfast, you can easily remove it with hydrogen peroxide. If your carpet, on the other hand, is not colorfast, try this remedy: Fill a spray bottle with hot water, adding a few drops of clear dishwashing liquid detergent. Shake and spray to saturate the stain. Then, cover with a piece of cloth—a clean washcloth or old pillow case will suffice—and get your steam iron! Place the hot iron over the stain for a minute or so. If you have to use the steam function, then do so. Keep ironing until the stain is transferred to the cloth!

Removing Glue

A proven method to remove glue—even when it's from those annoying price labels—is with a Q-tip and olive oil. Saturate the glue. Let it sit for 20 minutes. Wipe clean.

Removing Ink Stains from Your Hands

Ink on your fingers or palms again? Me too! Rub a little bit of sugar, which acts as a gentle exfoliate, and wash. The stain will be far easier to remove!

Cleaning Ceramic Tiles

Rubbing alcohol! It's true! Sprinkle rubbing alcohol on ceramic floors and then mop for a brilliant shine.

Ridding the Freezer of Smells

You have arrived and the refrigerator freezer . . . *smells*. How do you get rid of that awful scent? A cup of ground coffee will solve the problem. Leave a cup of ground coffee in your freezer and in a few days, the coffee will have absorbed all the unpleasant aromas.

Cleaning Reading Glasses

Why spend money on expensive cleaners for your eyeglasses when this will do: dab a bit of white toothpaste on both sides. Polish with a tissue. Not only will they be clean, but they won't fog up!

Cleaner Mirrors

If you combine 1/3 cup water with 1/4 cup rubbing alcohol, you'll have a potent mirror cleaner. Spray and wipe with newspaper or newsprint paper—a perfect use for the "Sociales" section of the *Diario de Yucatán*!

Shower Glass Doors

In the tropics water has much more limestone than elsewhere, doesn't it? One Easy, Breezy way of dealing with lime and alkaline deposits is time-tested: car wax! Glass is porous and car wax is formulated to protect car paint and glass. Clean you shower glass doors. Apply a layer of car wax. Polish. Car wax will reduce those water spots. Best part? This only needs to be done every six months.

Reduce Mold and Mildew

Have you noticed that eastern and northern walls tend to get more mold and mildew in the tropics? You have—if you're observant. One remedy is to combine one cup hydrogen peroxide, one cup water, and one teaspoon lemon juice. Using a spray bottle spray the backsplash in your kitchen and shower walls. No need to wipe or scrub anything. Routine spraying will kill and prevent both mold and mildew.

Soften Feet

Before bedtime, rub olive oil into the soles of your feet, toes, and heels. Then put on comfortable socks. You will be surprised how soft your feet's skin is in the morning. The olive oil dissipates into your skin, reducing calluses, and making your skin baby-soft!

Prevent Mosquitoes from Laying Eggs

Whether it's a bird bath, fountain or pool, a few drops of olive oil will keep mosquitoes from laying eggs in these bodies of water!

Brighten Leather Shoes

After you brush off dirt, dab a little olive oil. Smooth into your leather shoes for a spectacular shine!

Splinters Solution

In the tropics, everyone gets a splinter once in a while. Did you know that if you saturate the splinter and surrounding skin with vegetable oil in a few minutes you will be able to remove the splinter painlessly? Now you know!

Stubborn Soap Scum?

A time-tested remedy, you ask? Boil a bottle of white vinegar, reduce to simmer. Using gloves and a clean washcloth saturate the problem area. Let the vinegar soak the soap scum. Let dry overnight. It should wipe clean the following morning. And if it doesn't, use an old toothbrush!

Ring Around the Toilet—No More!

Banish ring around the toilet by pouring two cups of white vinegar every other week in your toilet water tank and letting it sit there for a few hours before you flush. Over time, the ring will disappear and form far slower going forward.

Clean Screws and Nails of Rust

Things do go better with Coca-Cola. Pour a Coke into a bowl and then soak nails or screws that are rusty. Another option: effervescent denture cleaners!

Homemade Wood Polish

Who needs Pledge? Combine two cups vegetable oil with two ounces lime juice. Use this as wood cleaner for months to come. Store in a cool, dry place.

Eliminate Small Scratches on Wood

It matters not how scratches appeared on wood surfaces—I'm sure the surveillance tape will settle the matter—but in the meantime, a little shoe polish will do the trick!

Eliminate Stains on Wood Surfaces

How? Diaper wipes work wonders. Use them to clean stubborn dirt or scuff marks on furniture, walls, and other surfaces.

Cleaning Stainless Steel

With everyone mad about the "industrial" and "stainless steel" look—as if everyone's kitchen should look like a restaurant's—the question arises often enough: "How do you keep your stainless appliances looking so spiffy, Cenote Sally?" The secret is this: baby oil. A dab on a soft cloth will do wonders to remove fingerprints and polish up that stainless steel so it looks perfect. Who knows when Jacques Pepin will show up to make you an omelet, right?

Carpet Stains

Spill some red wine on a carpet? Immediately pour salt or baking soda! The salt or baking soda will absorb the stain. Let it dry, then vacuum clean the salt—and the stain—away.

Clean Kitchen Sinks and Food Disposals Naturally!

For Easy, Breezy cleaning of your drains and pipes, once a month pour a cup of baking soda, used coffee grinds, and a cup of white vinegar down your kitchen sink drain, shower drain, and food disposal. Let warm water run. The effervescence of the baking soda and the acidic action of the vinegar will remove almost all the grease buildup, preventing problems!

End Water Deposit Build-Up

At the hacienda, we struggled with hard water for years, until I realized that lime and alkaline deposits were easily removed by soaking a paper towel or washcloth in white vinegar. If the hard water deposit is in the faucet itself, you can fill a coffee cup with vinegar and place it so that the faucet is submerged in the vinegar. Then let warm water run for about ten minutes.

Sage Advice

Did you know that sage kills bacteria? You do now! Grow sage in your garden. Then sprinkle a few leaves in your hamper, kitchen garbage, and everyday walking shoes. They will all keep fresher longer! That's Easy, Breezy, isn't it?

Scruff Marks

If someone's shoes have left a scruff mark on your floors, gently rubbing baking soda with a damp cloth is an excellent solution.

How Carpets Can Smell Fresh

In this tropical environment, it's difficult to keep carpets smelling fresh. Rather than spending a fortune on carpet fresheners, simply sprinkle carpets, area rugs, and upholstered chairs with baking soda. Let it sit for two hours, then vacuum!

Protect your Plants from Mildew

Mix ½ tablespoon baking soda, two cups soapy water, and two drops vegetable oil in a spray bottle. Spray both sides of your plants' leaves. You will have added an alkaline that inhibits mildew and other fungal spores from attacking your houseplants!

Baby Vomit Stains

Is someone's baby spitting up or worse yet, vomiting? If so, sprinkle baking soda to absorb the mess before it stinks up the place.

Cleaning Plastic

With plastic furniture all the rage—whatever happened to real wicker?—here's a simple cleaning solution: one quart water and four tablespoons white vinegar. You can use a spray bottle or a clean cloth.

Steel Wool Pads

Everyone has them—or has used them! But to prevent them from rusting, store them on a terracotta tray. Terracotta is designed to absorb water, drying out the pad, and preventing rust!

A Fresher Refrigerator

Going away for a few days? The best thing for making sure your refrigerator remains smelling fresh is simply to pour fresh coffee grounds in a couple of small dishes. Leave them on several shelves of your refrigerator. When you return, the refrigerator will smell fresh and splendid!

A Fresher Kitchen

If kitchen smells are a recurring problem, a simple solution is to wash four or five charcoal briskets in cool water and place them in a corner, or on top of a shelf, in your kitchen. The charcoal will absorb cooking odors on an ongoing basis.

Yellowed Sheets?

Yellowing sheets can be made bright once more by soaking them in a solution of warm water—with a cup salt and a cup baking soda added. Soak them overnight, then rinse well, and dry.

Cast Iron Bathtubs

1. Darling, I don't need you to tell me how popular these have become! Makes me wish I had one! If you do have one, here's how to clean it: baking soda dissolved in warm water to make a paste. Use a sponge to scrub it down! The baking soda will act as a gentle cleaning agent.

2. If your tub is vintage—and presumably has some rust—then you will need something stronger . . . and I mean using a pumice stone. Excellent for tough rust stains, pumice stones are porous and can handle the task. Keep the pumice stone wet throughout the cleaning process. Once the rust is removed rub lemon and salt into the entire stain. Let sit for 24 hours. The rust will transfer to the salt. It can then be gently washed away. Towel dry your tub to prevent future rust stains.

Cleaner Windshields

After your car is washed, have the windshield polished with car wax! It will repel dirt and make for far easier cleaning—just a simple garden hose.

Cleaner Windshield Wipers

Use rubbing alcohol to clean properly your windshield wipers!

Have Your Air Pressure Checked

Every time you fill up at your favorite gas station, ask the attendant to check the air. Under- or over-inflated tires wreck your gas mileage!

Empty the Trunk!

The more weight, the worse car mileage you will get. You don't need to lug around so much clutter in your trunk—it only costs you money!

Drive 10 percent Slower Than the Posted Speed Limit

Get in the habit of driving about 10 percent slower than the posted speed limit. An AAA study showed that drivers who adhere to this rule save over $130 USD in gas—and if it's true in the States, it has to be true here in the tropics as well!

Know Your Destination

MapQuest or Google or GPS before you head out! How many times have I gone past where I wanted to go, only to have to make a U-turn or back track?

Too often! Plan ahead.

Change Oil

Changing the oil every 4,500 kilometers (3,000 miles) or six months—whichever comes first—is a sure way of maximizing fuel efficiency. Now you know!

Temporary Life for Car Battery

Always have aspirin in the car. No, not for the headache your passengers will give you, but if your battery dies—two aspirins, which have acid, are likely to get the battery charged enough to start the engine—and get you to the nearest gas station. It works!

Drive Manual

This is an Easy, Breezy tip that will save you thousands of dollars over the course of your adult life: drive manual cars. The mileage is far better than automatic cars!

Protect Fine Linens

How? In the tropics, it's imperative you place a piece of wax paper on top of the fine linens. This will protect them from both mildew—and fading from strong sunlight.

Roll Up Windows

Rushing air is wonderful, but it produces a drag on the car making it use more gasoline or petrol. Roll up your windows, darling, and you will save hundreds over the course of the year while driving in the tropics.

Extend the Life of Car Seats

How? In the tropics, the sun can be unforgiving. If you have leather car seats, every three months polish baby oil into the leather—it will provide enough moisture to prevent the leather from cracking.

Floor Mats

In the tropics, beaches beckon all the time. A simple solution we found was using carpet samples from decorating stores and using them as catch-all floor mats during the times we would be constantly driving over to Sisal or the beaches that flank Progreso. At the end of the season, we discarded the sand-filled, dirty, and smelly carpets—and our "real" floor mats were fresh and clean!

Floor Mat Traction

How many times have, visiting friends along the beach, you've gotten stuck in the sand? Using the carpet floor mats suggested above can be used to create traction! Works wonders. Who cares if you ruin the seasonal carpet-turned-floor mat?

Plan Errands

Run all your errands around town in one trip. Hit the markets, banks, utilities, liquor stores, gourmet shops, and everything else at one time. You'll be more organized and you will save on fuel.

Buffing Up Bumpers

Try this, crazy as it seems! Get some lemon-infused mayonnaise and a soft cloth rag. Wipe and polish your bumpers with mayonnaise. Don't believe me? Try it—and you will see how easily grease (and even tar stains) will vanish!

Unwanted Bumper Stickers?

Time to remove the "I Was Bamboozled by Flamingo Lakes" or the "I Was Swindled by Brazos Abiertos" bumper stickers? You're not alone! Try this: using a hair dryer set at high, blow hot air over the bumper sticker until it softens. Then use vegetable oil as you remove from one corner. The vegetable oil will remove the adhesive.

Unwanted Window Decal?

For decals on glass, equal parts warm water and white vinegar will do the trick. Using a washcloth or sponge, saturate the decal. After about 20 minutes, it will be an Easy, Breezy task of removing the decal!

A Small Streak of Paint?

Oh, no! After saving at the big-box discounter, you get back to your car to find a small streak of paint where another car brushed up too close to you! An Easy, Breezy solution: spray WD-40 and wipe using a soft clean cloth. The paint will be gone.

Freshen Up the Trunk!

How? In the tropics, it's a clever resident who places a couple of sheets of dryer fabric softeners to keep funky odors out of your trunk.

Cheaper Car Rentals

How? Go to *Kayak.com* and make arrangements: it's possible to save up to 80 percent from booking directly with a travel agent or walking in off the street. These online bargains are available most of the year for the Cancún and Mérida markets.

Princess is Parched!

And I am confident you could use a potent potable just about right now. I think I'll have a . . .

PERNOD COCKTAIL

2 ounces Pernod
½ ounce water
1 dash Angostura bitters
¼ teaspoon sugar

Shake ingredients with ice. Strain into a chilled cocktail glass.

Read *The Sun Also Rises* by Ernest Hemingway. In Chapter 8, the Pernod cocktail takes center stage when it comes to drinks. Indeed, Jake and Bill order Pernod cocktails over dinner. "You'll be daunted after about three more pernods" is advice worth taking! But of course you knew that, didn't you?

Drink and read . . . responsibly!

WONDERFUL TIPS FOR A GOOD NIGHT'S SLEEP!

Did I tell you?

Sometimes I feel like Julie Andrews in *The Sound of Music*. Or perhaps I should feel like Rodgers & Hammerstein?

Who cares?

In the song, *I Have Confidence*, Julie Andrews blurts out these lines: "Strength lies in nights of peaceful slumber/When you wake up, Wake Up!"

Did I ever tell you about the time I was a houseguest at the gracious home of a friend in Colonia García Gineres—when they were also hosting Gabriel García Marquez? Well, to be in the company of that literary giant—and the stories he told about Mario Vargas Llosa, Isabel Allende, and Carlos Fuentes!

Let me tell you . . . *some other time* . . . right after I post a tell-all on Snapchat!

But enough about me and my name-dropping, let's move on to the matter at hand!

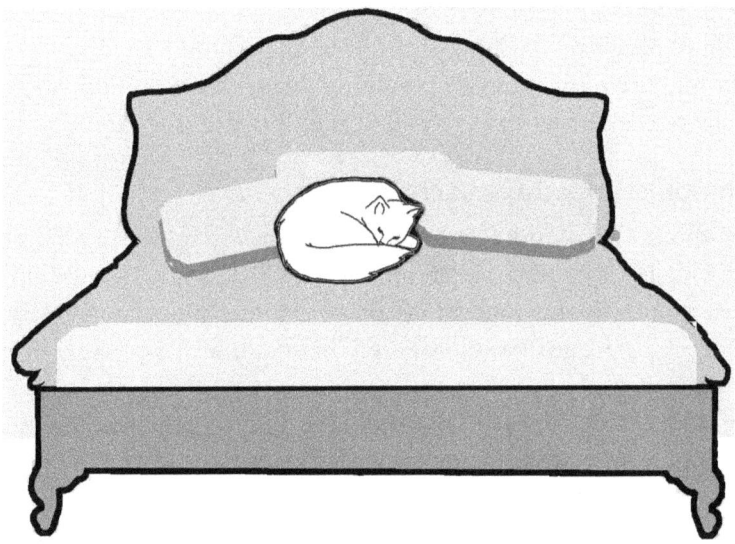

Wonderful Tips for a Good Night's Sleep

Make Your Bedroom a Sanctuary

No televisions, no tablets, no distractions! Keep your bedroom free of clutter and make it an inviting place. Invest in a good mattress for proper musculoskeletal support and make sure it is peaceful.

"Recondition" Your Bedroom

Your bed exists for two reasons alone: sleep and sex. (True, every room in the house can be used for sex, and some can be used for sleeping, but I digress.) If you psychologically associate your bedroom with sleep (and sex) it will be easier to get a good night's sleep.

Establish a Sleep-Wake Cycle

Don't eat in the bedroom. Don't read in the bedroom. Don't do anything on your iPhone (or whatever) in the bedroom. Go to sleep at the same hour and wake up at the same time. Habits form patterns and patterns form habits.

Do Not Eat or Drink Three Hours Before Sleep

The last morsel of the day and drink of the evening should take place a minimum of three hours before you go to sleep. The only exception is the taking of herbal tea. Remember that coffee and chocolate have caffeine. Remember that alcohol is processed as sugar and this makes it difficult to sleep. (Alcohol-induced sleep is not restful sleep, but you knew that, didn't you?)

Exercise During Waking Hours

Exercise is necessary and it's something that should be done every day. Avoid, however, strenuous exercise two hours before sleeping. Your body needs to enter a "sleep zone" of calmness when it "winds down" for the day.

Meditation or Breathing Exercises

Forget about the world for a while. Before you perform your evening ablutions, spend 15 or 20 minutes on mindfulness. Meditate. Breathe slowly and deeply. Close your eyes and concentrate on the senses. In tropical climates, enjoy the aroma, hear the fronds sway, listen to the wind, feel the breeze from your garden or terrace.

These habits will save you an untold fortune in prescription medicines, stress, anxiety, and treating ailments associated with the hurried lifestyles of the shortsighted and shallow.

Princess is Parched!

And I am confident you could use an appropriate digestive just about right now. I think I'll have . . .

TEA

Chamomile tea
Hot water

Soak tea bag in hot water until tea is flavorful to taste.

Read *The Last Good Country* by Ernest Hemingway. Everyone is eating prunes and drinking teas, presumably to have proper bowel movements and enjoy sound sleep!

Drink and read . . . responsibly!

EPILOGUE

Yes, now to the most riveting anecdote of all! How I became "Cenote Sally."

It all began with my love affair with *cenotes*. Aren't they wonderful? So cool and refreshing! And when you splash water at the ceilings, my, how the bats take flight!

My husband was always protective of me, fearing some mishap or other. He'd come over and say, "You've had your fun, now it's time to get out of there!"

This was during the time when he was attempting to perfect his Spanish. Of course we spoke Spanish in Cuba, but he always struggled with the *tú* command in the affirmative. You know what I mean: *hacer, haz; ir, ve; ser, sé*, etc. He wanted to say, *Sal del cenote*, or *Get out of the cenote*. Instead he said, *Salí del cenote*, meaning "I left the cenote." I knew what he meant to say, but when we had guests, I played dumb.

In 1968, we hosted Slim Keith when Jacqueline Kennedy was also in Yucatán. We all managed to arrange for a swim in one of the *cenotes*. It was a wonderful, clandestine treat for the beleaguered Mrs. Kennedy, still the object of pity over the assassination of her husband in Dallas years before. Of course my husband was paranoid about the entire thing. He kept coming over, saying, "*Salí del cenote*." Mrs. Kennedy, fluent in French and proficient in Spanish, just smiled.

"He's so wonderful," she said. "But '*Salí del cenote*,'? What's he trying to say?"

"He thinks my name is Sally!" I joked. "Sally del *cenote*."

Mrs. Kennedy laughed. "Then that makes you 'Cenote Sally,' doesn't it?"

"Cenote Sally, it is," Slim concurred.

Cenote Sally. My husband's poor Spanish. Mrs. Kennedy's wit.

We all laughed. Then it was time for lunch.

ADIOS, MI VIDA

I leave you with one parting wish. I hope that, in your life, you will have someone who loves you as much as my husband loved me. He would smile and tell me, "*Solo creo en los besos que me das.*" Wasn't he a doll?

Now, darling, I've kept my end of the bargain! Now keep yours!

Take these tips, incorporate them into your life! Yours will be a more holistic, green, and economical existence in this tropical paradise!

I have now empowered you to save thousands of dollars while enjoying an Easy, Breezy tropical lifestyle!

It's time to celebrate! Have a drink!

Read your Hemingway!

Save a small fortune!

It's Easy, Breezy!

ABOUT THE AUTHOR

Determined to bankrupt the Social Security Administration all by herself, Ms. Wentworth does not plan to die; she believes she has the stamina for immortality.

She lives in her gracious home, Hacienda Escondido in Yucatán, México.

INDEX

A

Accident Sites, pet, cleaning, 85
Across the River and Into the Trees, 87
Aebi, Caroline, 53
Age Spots, 70
ageratum, 34
aguas, 55, 57
aguas frescas, 55
Air Drying, 30
air freshener, 5, 56
Air Pressure, tires, 98
alarm clock, 55
algae, 42
alkaline, 7, 20, 94, 96-97
Allende, Isabel, 102
almond oil, 74
aloe vera, 68, 73
aluminum, 19, 38, 41
Álvarez, María Antonia Peregrino, 79
ammonia, 15, 36
Andrews, Julie, 102
antibiotics, 28
ants, 37, 41, 86
ants, keeping away from pet food bowl, 86
ants, keeping out of kitchen, 90
aphids, 38
Apples, 19, 63
Apricots, 63
artichokes, 63
ashtray, 14
avocado, 68-71
Avocado, 69
Avocado Oil, 70

B

baby oil, 48, 51, 96, 99
baby wipes, 84-85
Bach's Rescue Remedy, 84
bacon, 43
bacteria, 18, 20, 39, 55, 68-69, 71, 73, 76, 96
Bacteria, 20-21, 76
baking soda, 11-15, 19, 25-29, 42, 47-48, 50, 68, 73, 77, 90-91, 96-98
Baking Soda, 11
Baldwin, Alec, 88
banana peels, 38-39, 42
Bananas, 76
basket, 58
Bath, 70, 80
Bathing Cat, 85
Bathtub Stains, 50
Bathtubs, Cast Iron, 98
battery, 99
Battery, Car, 99
Beans, 12
beans, dried and canned, 63
bed, dog, 83
bedroom, 14, 45, 55, 77, 79, 103
Bedroom, 14, 103
beebalm. See horsemint
beef, 84
beer, 41, 60
bees, 36
beetles, 42
Belize, 4
Berries, 63
Berry Stains. See Stains, Berry
birdbath, 42

108

birds, 38
Bitter Buttons, 34
Bitters (vegetables), 76
bleaches, 20
blender, 13, 34, 57, 68
Blenders, 13
Blinds, 90
Blister, 69
Blood Pressure, 76
Blood Stains. *See* Stains, Blood
Body Scrub, 74, 78
Bones, Strengthen, 73
books, 1, 90
Books, mildew on, 90
Boxito, 1
Brand, Russell, 33
Brass, 19
Brass, tarnished, 93
Bread plates, 58
Breadboard, 58
Breath, 11, 68
Breath, dog, 85
British Honduras, 4
brownies, 55
Brushes, 12, 19
bugs, 91
bugs, keeping away from potted flowers, 91
bugs, keeping away from terrace, 91
Bugs, keeping out of bathroom, 91
Bumpers, car, buffing, 100
Buttons, 27
Byblos Restaurant, 76

C

Café De Bruxelles, Le, 53
calcium, 38, 72-73
Calluses, Reducing, 71
Campari & Gin, 5, 52
canapé, 58
Cancún, 50, 101

Candle Wax, 59
Candles, 58, 59
Canker Sores, 75
cannellini, 63
canola oil, 34
cantaloupe, 76
Capers, 63
Capote, Truman, 45
car, 14, 35, 50, 94, 98-100
Car Rentals, 100
Car Seats, 99
car wax, 35, 50, 94, 98
car, cleaner, 50
Carpet Stains. *See* Stains, Carpet
Carpets, 12, 97
Cars, 14
castor oil, 40
Cat, 80, 83, 85, 90
cat litter, 82, 85, 90
Cat Litter, 82
catnip, 34, 43
cats, 82-83, 85
cayenne, 34, 75, 84
Cedar, 83
Ceiling Fans. *See* Fans, Ceiling
cement, powder, 41
cenote, 105
Cenote Sally, 2-3, 92, 96, 105
cenotes, 105
Centerpiece, 58
Central Intelligence Agency, 1
ceramic floors, 93
Ceramic Tiles, 93
chalk, 37, 92
Champagne, 60
charcoal, 97
Chaya, 72
Cheese, 57, 60
Cheese knives, 57
Cheese, soft, grating, 62
cheeses, 4, 13, 57, 62

chemotherapy, 28
Chetumal, 4
Chetumalito, El, 4
Chewing, keep dogs from, 85
chicken, 43, 54, 84
chickpeas, 63
chiles, 63
chili, 56
Chlorine, 14
chocolate squares, 63
Chocolate Stains. *See* Stains, Chocolate
cigar, 26, 79
cigarettes, 26
cinnamon, 37, 41-42, 60, 86, 90
cinnamon bark oil, 42
citrodora, 34
citronella, 35
Clawing, Cat, 83
Closed Doors. *See* Puertas Cerradas
Clothes, 28-29, 77
clover, 41
cloves, 41
club soda, 27, 47, 61
coasters, 58
Coca-Cola, 48, 95
cockroaches, *See* roaches
Cocktail glasses, 57
Coffee, 7, 12-13, 18, 50, 63, 92
Coffee ,Vietnamese Style, 59
Coffee and Grass Stains. *See* Stains, Coffee and Grass
Coffee Grinds, 12
Coffee Makers, 13
Coffee Pots, 18
Coffee Stains. *See* Stains, Coffee, *See* Stains, Coffee
Coffee, Flavored, 60
Coffeemaker, 92
Coke, 25, 95
Coke, Diet, 25
cold cuts, 13

Collar, Ring Around the, 29
colorfast, 6, 20, 26-27, 47, 49, 85, 93
Combs, 12
Compost, 39
computer, 32, 76, 90
Computer Keyboards, cleaning, 93
Cooking Oil Stains. *See* Stains, Cooking Oil
Copper Cookware, 18
Coqui Coqui, 70
Cork, 59
corn starch, 12, 90
cornflower, 41
cornmeal, 37
Cornmeal, 63
cornstarch, 29, 37, 47, 80
Costco, 4, 49, 56
cotton ball, 8, 29, 51, 72, 91
cotton balls, 68, 71
Coughing, 73
Counter, 12, 21, 37
Couscous, 63
Cow Bitter, 34
crackers, 57
Crackers, 63
Cranberry Juice, 69
crayon marks, 14
crickets, 37
Crisco, 82
Crudités, 57
Cuba, 1, 32, 79, 105
cucumber, 68
cucumbers, 36
Cupcakes, 61
cuticles, 68, 72
Cutting Boards, 20

D

Daiquiri, 5, 44
dander, pet, 84
Dandruff, 71, 74

Dangerous Summer, The, 78
Decal, removing, 100
Decanter, 58
Decanters, 18
degreasing, 6
Denunciation, The, 15
Deodorant Stains. *See* Stains, Deodorant
deodorants, 7
Desk, cleaning, 93
Dessert plates, 58
detergent, 7, 8, 23- 27, 29-30, 35, 38, 40-41, 47-48, 50-51, 59, 93
devil's ivy, 38
Diario de Yucatán, 94
Dinner plates, 58
dishes, 12, 53, 59, 97
Dishwasher, 7
dog hair, 40, 81
Dog Toys, 86
dog, flying with, 84
dogs, 79, 80, 82- 85
Down, 25
drain, 12, 96
Drain, 13, 25
drains, 13, 96
driveway, 14
Dry Cleaning, 26
duct tape, 30, 69
Dust, 19, 90
dust mites, 42

E

Ear Infections, Dogs', 85
egg shells, 44
egg yolk, 67
egg yolks, 77
eggplant, 55
eggs, 38
Eggs, hard boiled, 62
eggs, mosquito, 95

Ek Balam, 56
endive, 76
Energy Booster, 75
Entertaining, 5, 53, 54
Entertainment Checklist, 57
Epsom salts, 36
Errands, 100
eucalyptus, 34-35, 70-71, 73, 78
exercise, 103
Exercise, 103
Exfoliate, 71, 74
Explore Yucatán, 56
eyeglasses, 94
Eyes, 75

F

fabric softener, 6, 7, 28, 36, 81, 83, 90
Fabric Softeners, 23
Facial Masks, 77
Fans, 7
Farewell to Arms, A, 9, 64
Feet, 69, 76, 94
Fennel, 72
fennel seed oil, 35
Fernández, Leopoldo, 79
ferns, 42
Fiberglass, 14
fingernails. *See* nails
Fingernails, 72
Fire Ants, 35
Flashlights, 63
flea eggs, 43
Fleas, 43, 81, 82, 83
flies, 36, 40, 43
Floor Mats, car, 99
flossflowers. *See* ageratum
Flour, 63
Flower Pots, 8
flower pots, protecting from dogs, 84
flowers, 35, 38-39, 42-43, 56, 64, 77, 91

Flowers, 39, 57, 91
Food Processors, 13
freezer, 42, 48, 58-62, 94
Freezer, ridding of smells, 94
French dressings, 29
Fruit Flies, 8
Fruit Trees, 38
fruit, tropical, 57
Fuentes, Carlos, 102
Fur, Pet, Tangled, 82

G

Garbage Cans, 13
Garbage Disposal, 18, 92
Garden, 5, 32, 34-35, 38-39, 42
garden tools, 35
Gardening Shears, 35
garlic, 6, 34, 40, 42, 54, 62, 64, 77, 91
Garlic press, 54
Gas, reducing, 72
Gasoline, 25
Gasoline Stains. *See* Stains, Gasoline
ghosts, 23
Gimlet, 5, 31
gin, 15, 22, 31, 39, 46, 52, 64, 87
Gin, 5, 15, 57
Gin & Tonic, 5, 15
Ginger, 75
ginger juice, 74
glasses, 58, 78
glassware, 7, 59
Glassware, 59
glue, 51, 93
Glue, removing. See
goblets, 58
Golden Buttons, 34
Google, 16, 84, 88, 98
GPS, 98
granola, 56
Grant, Cary, 32

Grape Juice Stains. *See* Stains, Grape Juice
Grapes, 57, 63
Grass Stains. *See* Stains, Grass
grasshoppers, 37
Grease Stains. *See* Stains, Grease
green tea, 68
greens, leafy, 91
Griffiths, Orion, 88, 89
grill, 37, 60
Grout, 12
Guacamole, 19
Gum, 7
Gum Stains. *See* Stains, Gum

H

Hair, 6, 12, 73, 74, 77, 88
hair dryer, 100
Hair, Lighten, 70
Hairspray, 28, 69
Hands, freshen, 61
Hangers, 30
hangers, clothes, 30, 55
hard water, 6, 7, 12, 20, 35, 96
Hard Water Stains. *See* Stains, Hard Water
Havana, 1, 32, 79
Hawks, Howard, 4, 32
Headache, 71
Hemingway, Ernest, 9, 15, 22, 31, 44, 45, 52, 64, 78, 87, 101, 104
Hemingway, Marina, 1
Hepburn, Audrey, 72
Home Depot, 1, 39
honey, 67, 73-74, 77
Hors D'oeuvres, 61
horsemint, 35
hosting, 55, 57, 79, 102
hot dogs, 56
Hot Oil (hair treatment), 77
houseplants, protecting from cats, 83
Hummus, 57

hydrogen peroxide, 11, 18, 26-27, 46, 47-50, 93-94

I

Ice Cubes, 61
Immersion blenders, 55
Immunity, Boost, 77
Ink Stains. *See* Stains, Ink,
insect, 8, 36, 60, 69, 91
Insect Bites, 69
Insect Repellent, 21, 60
insects, 1, 19, 36, 60, 91
ironing, 28, 59, 93
Irving R. Levine, 16
Islands in the Stream, 22, 44
Ivory, 20

J

Jams, making, 62
Jeans, 6, 30
Jewelry, 6, 11
Jews, 29
Juice, 21, 31, 50, 78

K

Kahlúa, 10
Kasha, 63
Kayak.com, 100
Keith, Kenneth, 4
Keith, Nancy, 4
Kennedy, Jacqueline, 45, 105
Ketchup Stains. *See* Stains, Ketchup
 Xocolatl, 56
kimchi, 76
Kitchen, 6, 12, 19, 21, 37, 54, 90, 96-97
Kitchen Smells. *See* Smells, Kitchen
Knives, 6
Kolozs, Carol, 10

L

La Lupita, 53
La Tremenda Corte, 79
Label Remover, 8
lace, 28, 47
Lace, 28
Lantern, Propane, 6
Last Good Country, The, 104
lavender, 41-42, 70-71, 73, 77, 81
Lavender, 41, 77
Lawn, 36
Lebanese Social Club, 76
lemon peels, 38
Lemonade, 57
Lemons, 5, 16-17, 57, 74, 83
Lentils, 63
Lever 2000 (deodorant soap), 82
Levine, Irvine R., 16
lime, 15, 17- 21, 27, 40, 42-44, 49, 71-72, 74, 94-96
Limes, 57
linen, 25
linens, 1, 26, 47, 56, 99
linens, antique, 47
Linens, protect, 99
linoleum, stains on, 50
Lint, 30
Lip Treatment, 73
Lipstick Stains. *See* Stains, Lipstick
Litter Box, cleaning, 85
Litter Boxes, 82, 85
Llosa, Mario Vargas, 102
lotions, 6

M

mandolin, 55
Mango, 61
Manicures, 77
MapQuest, 98
marble, 92

Marble, cleaning, 92
marigolds, 34
Maroma, 34
Marquez, Gabriel García, 102
Martin, Andrea, 88
Martini, 5, 64
Massage, Facial, 76
mattress, 14, 103
mayonnaise, 72, 91, 100
Mazola, 91
meat tenderizer, 28
Meat, browning, 62
Meats, 62
Medianoche (sandwich), 55
Meditation, 103
Mérida, 1, 4, 16, 23, 36, 45, 53, 56, 77, 84, 101
Mezcal, 57
Miami, 4, 66, 79
mice, 40, 90
microwave, 19-21, 92
Microwave, Cleaning, 92
Microwaves, 20
Miguel Bretos, 16, 17
mildew, 1, 13, 18, 26, 47, 90, 94, 97, 99
Milk, 13, 14
mint, 40, 68, 75
Mint, 68
Mirrors, 94
mojito, 68
mold, 90, 94
Mold, 94
moles, 41
Mosquitoes, 1, 34, 43, 95
moth balls, 36, 82
Mugwort, 34
Museum of the City, 4
mushrooms, 63, 68
Muslims, 29
mustard, 56, 63
Mustard Stains. *See* Stains, Mustard

N

Nail Care, 72
Nail Clippers, 73
nail polish remover, 28
nails, 68, 70, 72, 95
Nails, whiten, 70
Napkins, 57-58
Napkins, White, 24
nasturtiums, 40
National Public Radio, 85
Nectar (restaurant), 53
neem, 34, 36, 56
Negroni, 87
Nervous Pets, 84
Newport, Rhode Island, 88
newsprint, 40, 42, 94
nitrogen, 39
NPR. *See* National Public Radio
Nuts, 61
nuts, mixed, 57

O

oatmeal, 68-69, 71, 77
Oil Stain, Suntan, 25
Oil Stains. *See* Stains, Oil
Oil, change, 99
olive oil, 18-19, 63, 67, 72, 74, 77, 93-95
Olive oil, 71
Olive paste, 63
olives, 76
Olives, 57, 63, 64
Olvera, Nancy Walker, 39
onion, 34, 38, 48, 61, 64
onions, 56, 62
Onions, Red, 61
opossums, 36
oral care, canine, 84
orange, 38
orange peels, 28, 34, 37-38, 60, 87
orange, sour, 61

orange, Valencia, 61
oranges, 34, 76, 78, 92
Orphans, 88
Oven Stains, *See* Stains, Oven
Oxxo, 56

P

Page, Bettie, 71
Paint streak on car, removing, 100
Painted, 14, 19
Paley, Babe, 32
pan, cast-iron, 92
Pancakes, 61
panini press, 55
Pantry, 63
papaya, 71
parchment, 55
pasta, 42, 63
Paws, 84
Peaches, 63
Pears, 63
pecans, 61
Pedicures, 71, 77
Pemex, 56
pencil marks, 14
Pepica's, 78
Pepin, Jacques, 96
pepper, black, 28
peppermint, 75
peppermint oil, 37, 75
Pepsi, 25
Perfume, 72
Perfumes, extend life of, 70
Pernod Cocktail, 101
Perry, Katy, 33
perspiration, 7, 28, 29, 49, 80
Perspiration Stains. *See* Stains, Perspiration
Pet Hair, 81
Petrol, 25
picnic, 56

Picnic Lunch, 56
pillows, 14, 25, 82
Pillows, 25
Piñata, 59
Pineapples, 63
Pippin, 88
pistachios, 61
pitcher, 18, 58, 78
Pitchers, 18
Place cards, 58
plants, potted, 34, 39
plaster of Paris, 37
plastic, 8, 14, 24, 42, 60, 82, 97
Plastic Containers, 14
Plastic Wrap, 60
Plastic, Cleaning, 97
Platos Rotos, 53
Playlist, 57
Pledge, 95
Plums, 63
polenta, 63
pool, 10, 34, 57, 79-80, 90, 95
Pools, Cleaner, 90
potassium, 39, 42, 76
potatoes, 42, 55
Potted Plants. *See* Plants, potted
Poultry, 62
Prescription Medicines, 28
pressure washer, 51
Produce, keeping clean and crisp, 91
Propane. *See* Lantern, Propane
Prune Juice, 69
Puertas Cerradas, 53
pumice, 98

Q

Q-tip, 36, 93

R

raccoons, 40
radicchio, 76
Radishes, 61
reading lamp, 55
Reagan, Nancy, 32
Refrigerator, 13, 18-19, 60, 70, 94, 97
Reguera, Ana de la, 10
Relish Stains. *See* Stains, Relish
rice, 20, 35, 64, 92
roaches, 37
roast, 43
Robertson, Merle Greene, 76
Rockwell, Norman, 30
Rodgers & Hammerstein, 102
Rolling Pin, 60
Rolls, 60
Rooms, 19
rooms, guest, 64
Rosas & Xocolatl, 10
rosemary, 41, 76-78
roses, 43
rubber gloves, 15, 35, 48, 51
rubbing alcohol, 29, 36, 49, 69, 72-73, 91, 93-94, 98
Rugs, area, 12
rust, 35, 49, 97, 98
Rust, 35, 95
Rust Stains. *See* Stains, Rust
Ryan, Irene, 88

S

sage, 73, 96
Salad Dressing Stains. *See* Stains, Salad Dressings
Salad plates, 58
salad spinner, 55
Salami, 57
Salsa Stains. *See* Stains, Salsa, *See* Stains, Salsa
salt, 11, 13, 18-20, 27, 35, 48- 51, 59, 68-71, 73-74, 78, 92, 96, 98
Sam's Club, 4
Sangria, 5, 78
Sanitizer, Hand, 73
sap, removing from hands, 43
Sauna, 70
scissors, kitchen, 54
Scorpions, 1, 17-18
Scratches on Wood, hiding, 91
screws, 95
Scruff Marks, 96
Scuff Marks, 28
seeds, 42, 68, 72
seeds, storing, 42
Serving platters, 58
Seven-Up (7-Up), 39
shampoo, 12, 25, 56, 71, 74, 77
Shaw, Fiona, 88
Sheets, 29-30
Sheets, yellowed, 97
shoe polish, 91, 95
Shoe Polish Stains. *See* Stains, Shoe Polish
Shoe Smells, 28
Shoelaces, 28
shoes, 21, 28, 69, 95-96
Shoes, 95
Short Happy Life of Francis Macomber, The, 31
Shower, 6, 18
Shower Doors, 94
Siestas, 57
silk, 25
silverfish, 41
Silverware, 58
Sinks, 19, 96
Skin, 67, 73, 84
skin, dry, 67
skin, moisturize, 70
skin, oily, 67
skin, stressed, 68

skin, sunburned, 68
skin, toning, 71
Sleep-Wake Cycle, 103
Slim, 4, 105
slugs, 41, 44
Smithsonian Institution, 16
snails, 44
Soap Scum, 95
Soda, 58
soda maker, 55
Solis, Roberto, 53
Sorbetería Colón, 56
Sore Throat, 73
sorrel tea, 75
Sound of Music., The, 102
sour cream, 73
Sour Cream Stains. *See* Stains, Sour Cream
Speed Limit, 98
spiders, 38, 41, 43
Splinters, 95
Sponges, 6
spray bottle, 6, 17, 19, 21, 34, 37-38, 50, 83, 90-91, 93-94, 97
squash, 55
stainless steel, 12, 19, 92, 96
Stainless Steel, 12, 96
Stains, Berry, 47
Stains, Blood, 28, 47
Stains, Carpet, 20, 93
Stains, Chocolate, 47
Stains, Coffee, 48, 50
Stains, Cooking Oil, 48
Stains, Deodorant, 48
Stains, Gasoline, 48
Stains, Grape Juice, 50
Stains, Grass, 48
Stains, Grease, 29
Stains, Gum, 48
Stains, Hard Water, 12
Stains, Ink, 28, 48, 93
Stains, Ketchup, 26, 49

Stains, Lipstick, 49
Stains, Mustard, 49
Stains, Oil, 14
Stains, Oven, 92
Stains, Perspiration, 49
Stains, Relish, 27
Stains, Rust, 49
Stains, Salad Dressing, 29
Stains, Salsa, 26, 49
Stains, Shoe Polish, 49
Stains, Sour Cream, 27
Stains, Suede, 7
Stains, Syrup, 26
Stains, Tea, 27
Stains, Tobacco, 50
Stains, Wine, 27, 50
Stains, Worcestershire Sauce, 27
Steak knives, 58
steamer, bamboo, 55
Steel Wool Pads, 97
Sticker Residue, removing from leather, 51
Stomach, Upset, 21
Suede Stains. *See* Stains, Suede
Sugar, 64
Suitcases, 13
Sun Also Rises, The, 101
sunscreen, 6
Suntan Oil Stain. *See* Stain, Suntan Oil
Sweets, 74
Syrup Stains. *See* Stains, Syrup

T

Tabasco, 40, 41
Tablecloth, 58
tablecloths, 47
tailors, 77
talcum powder, 28-29, 82, 85, 90
Tar Removal, 8
Tea, 6, 27, 39, 75, 104
Tea Stains. *See* Stains, Tea

Tea Stains, removing from porcelain, 51
tea, Oolong, 75
Teas, 58, 64, 75
teeth, 68, 73, 75, 84
teeth, dogs, 84
television, 79, 88, 90
Tenderizer, Meat, 13
tennis ball, 90
tennis balls, 25
Tennis Balls, 90
Tennis Shoes, 21
tequila, 39
Terrace, 5, 32, 34, 37, 40, 91
Testament of Mary, The, 88
Thousand Island dressings, 29
ticks, 36
Tire Marks, 50
Tobacco, 26
Tobacco Smells, 26
Tobacco Stains. *See* Stains, Tobacco
Toilet, 20
Toilet, ring, 95
tomato leaves, 37
Tomatoes, 63
tomatoes, canned, 63
tomatoes, sun-dried, 64
Toña la Negra. *See* Álvarez, María Antonia Peregrin
Tonic, 58
toothbrush, 7, 12, 48, 73, 95
toothpaste, 48, 56, 94
Toothpicks, 58
Tortilla, 64
Tortillas, 58
Towels, 26, 30
Tres Patines, 79
trisodium phosphate, 51
True at First Light, 52
Trunk, car, 98
Trunk, car, freshen, 100
T-Shirts, 7

tuna, oil-packed, 63
Tweezers, 73

U

undergarments, 28

V

Vacuum Cleaners, 14
vanilla extract, 60, 64, 91
Varicose Veins, 71
Vases, 35
vegetable oil, 50, 91, 95, 97, 100
Vegetable peelers, 54
Vegetables, 13, 18, 62
Veracruz, 1, 79
Vereen, Ben, 88
Vermouth Panaché, 5, 9
Vertigo, 68
vinegar, 5-8, 12-13, 15, 18, 21, 24, 26, 28, 30, 35, 47-48, 50-51, 64, 74, 85-86, 91-93, 95-97, 100
Vinegar, 4, 5, 8, 64
vinegar, cider, 8, 35
Vital Organs, 75
vodka, 39
Vodka, 58
vomit, baby, 97

W

Waffles, 62
walnuts, 61
Wart, 69
Washing Machine, 7
Wasp Stings, 8
wasps, 43
water, bottled, 63
Water, Healthy, 74
wax paper, 26, 99
weeds, 38, 40

Wentworth, Eunice, 2, 107
White Lady, 5, 22
Wikileaks, 32, 33
wilting, 18, 39
Windows, 20, 37, 43
Windows, car, 99
Windshield Wipers, 98
Windshields, 98
wine, 20, 27, 37, 45-46, 59, 62, 64, 78, 96
Wine Stains. *See* Stains, Wine
winter creeper, 38
witch hazel, 34
Wood, 4, 18-19, 91, 95
Wood floors, 91
Wood Polish, 95
Wood, stains on, 95
Wood, water stains on, 91
wool, 25
Worcestershire Sauce Stains. *See* Stains, Worcestershire Sauce
wrist, 68
Wrists, 74

X-Y-Z

Y2K, 66
yogurt, 68, 74, 76
Yucatán, 1-2, 4-5, 10, 16, 29-30, 39, 55, 79, 105, 107

www.ingramcontent.com/pod-product-compliance
Lightning Source LLC
Chambersburg PA
CBHW081355040426
42451CB00017B/3459